Buddhist Faith and Sudden Enlightenment

SUNY Series in Religious Studies
Robert C. Neville, EDITOR

BUDDHIST
FAITH
and
SUDDEN
ENLIGHTENMENT

Sung Bae Park

Center for Religious Studies
State University of New York at Stony Brook

State University of New York Press

ALBANY

To Chin-hoe

152564

Published by State University of New York Press, Albany

© 1983 State University of New York

All rights reserved

Printed in the United States of America

For information, address State University of New York Press, State University Plaza, Albany, N.Y., 12246

Library of Congress Cataloging in Publication Data

Park, Sung Bae.
    Buddhist faith and sudden enlightenment.

    (SUNY series in religious studies)
    Bibliography: p. 169
    Includes index.
    1. Faith (Buddhism) 2. Enlightenment (Zen Buddhism) I. Title. II. Series.
BQ 4345.P37   1983   294.3′44   82-10459
ISBN 0-87395-673-7
ISBN 0-87395-674-5 (pbk.)

10   9   8   7   6   5   4   3   2

Contents

Preface

One of the most radical developments in the history of East Asian Buddhism was the Ch'an tradition of "sudden enlightenment." From this development arose the famous debate of "sudden enlightenment" versus "gradual cultivation." From the philosophical point of view, one must ask: "How is sudden enlightenment possible?" The answer I arrived at is that sudden enlightenment becomes possible through the awakening of what is termed in Korean Buddhism a *patriarchal faith*, defined as an affirmation that "I am Buddha."

Throughout this writing I have tried to focus on the interrelationship between faith, practice, and enlightenment in East Asian Mahāyāna Buddhism, concentrating especially on the connection between sudden enlightenment and patriarchal faith. The approach I have taken is neither historical nor philological, but rather philosophical. It also corresponds to my personal experiences as a Sŏn (Chinese: Ch'an; Japanese: Zen) monk of the Chogye order in Korea, which was heavily influenced by the integration of Sŏn meditation and Kyo (scriptural study) established by Chinul (1158-1218). Specifically, as a Sŏn monk residing at Haeinsa (Ocean Seal Monastery), located at South Kyŏngsang province in Korea, I was trained in the Lin-chi tradition of *kong'an* (Chinese: *kung-an*; Japanese: *kōan*) meditation. Therefore, my discussion of Buddhist faith, practice, and enlightenment often reflects this orientation. Nonetheless, because of its highly general nature, I consider my system of interpretation to be useful as a tool for analyzing all schools of East Asian Mahāyāna Buddhism.

A basic motivation for my writing this kind of book has been to show the striking difference existing between doctrinal and patriarchal faiths in terms of two different kinds of Buddhists at the level of everyday life. One group attempts to grasp Buddhism in a conceptual way, whereas the other group enters into Buddhism in its existential dimensions, through a "leap of faith," to borrow Sören Kierkegaard's famous phrase.

What impressed me most when I first joined the Korean Monastery was that the faith of Chosil Sunim, the spiritual leader in the monastery, was quite different from that of ordinary monks. Chosil Sunim did not have any intention of making his followers obtain enlightenment. Rather, he firmly believed that all sentient beings are already perfect Buddhas. Furthermore, he believed in a kind of grace (Korean: *kap'i*) dispensed by Buddhas and Bodhisattvas.

It was extremely difficult for me to accept this unbelievable fact. Since then, I have struggled unceasingly with the notion of Buddhist faith in the Ch'an tradition of East Asia. This book can therefore be described as an interim report of my inquiry into the existential dimensions of Buddhism as seen especially in the lives of enlightened patriarchs.

For writing this book I owe many people. First of all, my gratitude should be addressed to the many monks in Korean monasteries who put much effort in leading me toward a right direction and bringing about many radical changes in my life. In terms of academic discipline, I would like to express my special gratefulness to Dr. Lewis Lancaster, University of California at Berkeley, who gave me constant suggestions for revision of my manuscript. Since I joined the Center for Religious Studies at the State University of New York at Stony Brook in 1977, the various center faculty members, especially Professors Thomas J. J. Altizer and Robert C. Neville, as well as my colleagues, Drs. Patrick Heelan, Peter Manchester, David Dilworth, Antonio T. de Nicolás, and Christopher Chapple have enabled me to see the importance of philosophical dialogue in the area of East-West comparative religions. I cannot forget the very generous arrangements made by the Venerable Master Hsüan-Hua, the abott of Tathāgata Monastery in the City of Ten Thousand Buddhas, Talmage, California, who graciously provided me with an excellent retreat situation for purposes of research and writing for an entire month in the summer of 1981. Also, I would like to thank Drs. Ron Epstein of Dharma Realm University, Carl Bielefeldt of Stanford University, and Kenneth Inada, State University of New York at Buffalo, for their careful readings of my manuscript and valuable suggestions.

For the completion of the book, I am very grateful to the Institute for Advanced Studies of World Religions, especially Dr. C. T. Shen, the president of the Institute; Drs. Richard A. Gard, and Christopher George, the directors of the Institute; Mrs. Hannah Robinson, and Mrs. Lena Yang, the Institute librarians; all of them have always granted me a special arrangement to use the Institute facilities and library which has one of the best collections of Buddhist texts in the United States. Also, my warmest appreciation must be addressed to Dr. Steve Odin who assisted me with the most painstaking jobs for my book from beginning to end and to my students In-sook Han and Jeff Seibel who worked on the bibliography, index, as well as proofreadings.

Finally, but most sincerely, I would like to express my deep feeling and hearty thanks to Chin-hoe, my wife, whose never yielding support and understanding have given me strength. To her I dedicate this book.

Sung Bae Park
Center for Religious Studies
State University of New York at Stony Brook

Introduction

It is now well known that Buddhism is a religion of meditation and of enlightenment; yet few are aware that it is also a religion of faith. Without right faith, no practice can be initiated and no enlightenment attained in Buddhism. Why then, is Buddhism not known as a religion of faith? Westerners regard it as a nontheistic religion and, as such, one that requires no faith. Unlike Western theistic religions, which are based on a dualistic subject–object structure, as expressed in the "faith in ———" construction (e.g. "faith in *God*"), the East Asian tradition of Mahāyāna Buddhism is based on a nondual *t'i-yung*, or "essence–function" construction. According to East Asian Mahāyāna Buddhism, faith does not require an object; rather, it is a natural function (*yung*) of one's own (originally enlightened) Mind, understood as *t'i*, or "essence." Consequently, the concept of faith in East Asian Mahāyāna Buddhism represents a challenge to Western theistic religions and demonstrates that there are serious alternatives to the dualistic "faith in ———" construction.[1]

In the tradition of East Asian Mahāyāna Buddhism, the role of faith is central. The Hua-yen school, which is based on the *Hua-yen ching*, or *Flower Adornment Scripture*, is usually regarded as having achieved the highest degree of philosophical systematization in East Asian Buddhism. As interpreted by such patriarchs of the Hua-yen school as Fa-tsang (643-712) and Ch'eng-kuan (738-840), the *Hua-yen ching* outlines a scheme of fifty-two stages in the career of bodhisattvas. The first ten of these are called the "ten faiths" (*shih-hsin*), and the last stage of "marvelous enlightenment" (*miao chiao*) is defined as the "perfection of faith." This structure therefore reflects a primacy of faith in the Hua-yen system of thought.[2]

In the two major traditions of East Asian Buddhist practice, Ch'an and Pure Land, faith again has a primary role. The Ch'an, or meditation, school understands faith to be a state of conviction or resoluteness that keeps one firmly rooted in practice, whereas the Pure Land school understands faith to be total reliance on Amida Buddha's forty-eight vows of compassion as the sole means of being born in Pure Land. Therefore, whereas Ch'an faith is a form of "self-power" (Japanese: *jiriki*), Pure Land faith is a form of "other-power" (*tariki*). Yet, despite this crucial distinction, faith in both cases is considered to be the primary cause of salvation.

Although it has an important role in East Asian Mahāyāna Buddhism, the concept of faith has been largely neglected by modern Buddhologists, not only in the West but in the East as well. Even contemporary Japanese Buddhist scholarship, with its enormous output of scholarly work, has produced no major *systematic* studies of Buddhist faith except the other-power faith practiced in Pure Land Buddhism.[3] The self-power faith supported by Ch'an remains almost completely unexplored. Faith is discussed with some frequency in the traditional East Asian commentaries in relation to important passages in the *sūtra*s that mention faith. However, none of these commentaries presents a systematic doctrine of faith, and none raises any important critical questions about faith. Thus, the concept of faith still represents a major gap in our understanding of East Asian Mahāyāna Buddhism.

Why has faith been neglected in modern Buddhist scholarship? One reason is that, although many Buddhist *sūtra*s emphasize the importance of faith, they say very little about the nature of faith, and even that tends to be obscure. The *Ta-ch'eng ch'i-hsin lun*, or *Treatise on Awakening Mahāyāna Faith*,[4] which is the key Mahāyāna Buddhist text on the subject of faith, contains no extensive discussion or analysis of faith, and whatever it does provide — for example, extollations of faith in the "three treasures" (i.e., Buddha, Dharma, and Saṃgha) or the means for perfecting one's faith through the "six perfections" (*pāramitās*) — is usually very traditional. Furthermore, traditional East Asian Buddhist commentators apparently assumed that faith was not something to be systematically analyzed, critically questioned, or objectified by reason, but something to be aroused in one's heart and lived by.

To begin closing this large gap in the field of Buddhist studies, I have attempted to write a systematic book on the dynamics of Mahāyāna Buddhist faith. Rather than adopt a philological and historical approach, I have analyzed the structure of Mahāyāna Buddhist faith on philosophical grounds. I have also raised various critical questions about the nature of faith. For example, what is the relation between faith and salvation in Buddhism? Buddhism is not simply a philosophy of life; it is also a religion with soteriological concerns. Yet there always exists a kind of gap between theory and practice. What bridges this gap? It is faith! The act of arousing faith allows one to advance from a merely intellectual understanding of Buddha's teachings to the levels of practice and salvation. For this reason, the initial act of awakening faith is the most difficult to achieve. This, perhaps, is why faith is the most neglected topic in all of modern Buddhist scholarship.

In this study I have called attention to a crucial distinction between two radically different kinds of

[3]

Buddhist faith established by the celebrated Korean monk Chinul (1158–1210): patriarchal faith (Korean: *choshin*; Chinese: *tsu-hsin*) and doctrinal faith (Korean: *kyoshin*; Chinese: *chiao-hsin*).[5] Whereas doctrinal faith is the belief that "I can *become* Buddha," patriarchal faith is the affirmation that "I am *already* Buddha." Even within traditional East Asian Buddhism itself, the notion of patriarchal faith is not well known. The kind of faith usually discussed by Buddhist scholars is doctrinal faith, or the faith that one has the potential to become Buddha through a gradual process of faith, understanding, practice, and enlightenment. However, against this tradition I argue that patriarchal faith is a much more potent idea than doctrinal faith, having important consequences at the levels of practice and enlightenment.

The issue of patriarchal faith versus doctrinal faith provides a new vantage point for understanding one of the most controversial debates in East Asian Buddhism: sudden enlightenment versus gradual enlightenment. Whereas the doctrinal faith that "I can become Buddha" is the basis of gradual enlightenment, the act of arousing a patriarchal faith that "I am already Buddha" is the basis of sudden enlightenment. Thus, I have raised another important question: Is sudden enlightenment possible? My contention is that, if sudden enlightenment is possible at all, then it is achieved only by the arousal of a patriarchal faith. I have also reconsidered the more traditional debate between self-power faith (as in Ch'an) and other-power faith (as in Pure Land) from the standpoint of the debate between patriarchal and doctrinal faith in order to show that patriarchal faith can be approached from either the direction of self-power or that of other-power.

Another philosophical problem I have considered is that of nonbacksliding faith (*pu t'ui hsin*) versus backsliding faith (*t'ui hsin*). I have argued here that right faith (*cheng hsin*) in Buddhism is equivalent to patriarchal faith. In East Asian Buddhism, the criterion for right faith is usually that it be nonbacksliding or nonretrogressive. Therefore, I have raised the question: Is a nonbacksliding faith possible? Again, my contention is that, if a nonbacksliding faith is possible, it is possible only on the basis of the arousal of a patriarchal faith, or the affirmation that "I am Buddha."

However, if it is true that "I am already Buddha," why should I perform spiritual practice? This problem is well illustrated by the Hua-yen theory of fifty-two stages, according to which all fifty-two stages in the life of a bodhisattva "interpenetrate," so that the last stage of marvelous enlightenment is already contained in the first stage of initial faith. However, if the first stage of initial faith is already identical to the last stage of marvelous enlightenment, why are the fifty stages in between necessary? In response to this question, I have examined the theory of sudden enlightenment and gradual practice developed by Tsung-mi (780–841), who was a patriarch of both the Hua-yen and Ch'an sects, as well as by Chinul. According to this theory, sudden enlightenment must always *precede* gradual practice, or it is not true practice. Thus, all fifty-two stages of the bodhisattva's career are implicit in an act of patriarchal faith, as its true content.

Finally, if one becomes convinced that a true Mahāyāna Buddhist patriarchal faith is indeed possible, one must then raise the most pressing question of all: How can one arouse patriarchal faith?

In this study I will analyze faith as having three components: faith, practice, and enlightenment. Buddhist faith is characterized by its inseparability from practice and enlightenment. One cannot discuss Buddhist faith without also discussing Buddhist practice and enlightenment. Thus, I have divided this book into three parts corresponding to each of the components of faith. However, consistent with the theory of patriarchal faith, I have argued that faith is not a mere preliminary to practice and enlightenment, as it is assumed to be in the theory of doctrinal faith; rather, faith *is* practice and practice *is* enlightenment. Practice and enlightenment are implicit in an act of faith as its content. Therefore, patriarchal faith is both the alpha and omega of the process of salvation.

Another gap in the field of Buddhist studies which I have tried to fill is the serious lack of doctrinal discussion of *kung-an* (Korean: *kong'an*; Japanese: *kōan*) practice or "questioning mediation" in the Ch'an tradition of East Asian Mahāyāna Buddhism. I have suggested that faith is the missing link in our understanding of *kung-an* practice. More particularly, I have argued that the practice of *kung-an* or questioning meditation involves a dynamic interplay between faith and doubt, or a dialectical tension between affirmation and negation, which becomes resolved in the process of questioning itself.

In this respect I would like to relate my position to the Kyoto School of Japan, founded by the great philosopher Kitarō Nishida, which includes such distinguished members as Keiji Nishitani, Yoshinori Takeuchi and Masao Abe.[6] The Kyoto school has done much to clarify the role of "Great Doubt" (Japanese: *daigi*) in the process of realizing Great Enlightenment. For instance, in his outstanding work called *What is Religion?*, Keiji Nishitani describes with great depth the way in which Great Doubt is the pressing of our doubt to its extreme limits, so as to extinguish our ego into the abyss of *nihilum*, i.e., the ground of absolute nothingness. This experience, as Keiji Nishitani says, is called the Great Death in Zen Buddhism. In this experience, according to him, the distinction between the doubter and the doubted collapses into a "great doubting-mass," which is a deep existential awareness of an unfathomable *nihilum*.[7]

Keiji Nishitani quotes the so-called "Takusui Sermons" to show the uniqueness of the Great Doubt in his English version of *What is Religion?* The quotation says:

> The method to be practiced is as follows: you must doubt concerning the subject in you which hears all voices. All voices are heard just now because there certainly is in you a subject that hears. Although you hear voices with ears, the holes of the ears are not the subject that hears. If they were, dead men also would hear voices . . . . You must doubt deeply again and again, asking yourself what could be the subject of hearing. Don't mind the various illusive thoughts and ideas that may occur to you. Only doubt more and more deeply, with all the gathered might of your entire self, without aiming at or expecting anything beforehand, without even intending to be enlightened, but also without intending not to intend to be enlightened; and being within your breast like a child . . . . But, however you go on doubting, you will find it impossible to know the subject that hears. Then you must still more deeply explore just there, where it is not to be known. Doubt deeply in a state of single-mindedness, looking neither before nor after, right nor left, becoming wholly like a dead man and becoming unaware even of your own person being there. When this method is practiced more and more deeply, you will come to a state of being totally absent-minded and vacant. Even then, you must raise up the great doubt, "What is the subject that hears?" and must doubt further, being all the time wholly like a dead man. And after that, when you are aware no more of your being wholly like a dead man, are no more conscious of your procedure of "great

doubting" and become, yourself, through and through a great doubt-mass, there will come all of a sudden a moment when you come out into transcendence called the Great Enlightenment, as if you woke up from a great dream, or as if you, being completely dead, suddenly revived.[8]

Although this quotation provides us with a glimpse of various aspects of the Great Doubt and its relation to the Great Death and Great Enlightenment, it fails to demonstrate how one can actually come to acquire the Great Doubt. In other words, Nishitani in general fully explores the importance of the Great Doubt in a religious sense, but he does not point out why people do not have this Great Doubt. He just keeps on saying, as do the Zen masters: "Doubt, doubt, doubt." The actual tual dynamics involved in the *kōan* process of doubting are never articulated in a philosophical way.

Therefore, in criticism of the Kyoto school, I feel that they have neglected the primacy of faith and its dialectical interplay with Great Doubt in the *kung-an* practice of questioning meditation. Without the dialectical tension between doubt and faith, the ego can never break apart and return to the ground of absolute nothingness. Thus, whereas I greatly admire the Kyoto school's philosophical approach to Buddhism, their engagement of the Western tradition, as well as their emphasis on the experience of Great Doubt, I have attempted to add a new dimension to the understanding of *kung-an* practice by developing the dialectical tension between Great Doubt and Great Faith which results in Great Enlightenment.[9]

Part One
Faith

BUDDHA
Cave monastery, Kyong-ju, Korea. Carved during the Silla
Dynasty, eighth century A.D.

Chapter One
The Primacy of Faith
in Buddhism

Traditional Buddhist literature is filled with references to a "primacy of faith" in religious life. Nāgārjuna's encyclopedic *Ta-chih-tu lun*, or *Treatise on the Perfection of Great Wisdom*, for which he is often called the Patriarch of Eight Schools, expresses this primacy of faith as follows:

> In the great sea of Buddha's teaching, Faith is that by which one can enter; Wisdom is that by which one can be saved.[1]

This statement appears in Nāgārjuna's explanation of the words *evam mayā śrutam*, "Thus I have heard," which appear at the beginning of all Buddhist *sūtra*s. Nāgārjuna continues:

> If one has a pure faith then one can enter the Buddha's teachings. If one does not have faith, one is not able to enter the Buddha's teachings. Those who do not have faith in Buddha say "not thus." This is the work of disbelief. Those who believe say "thus."[2]

Since faith is the *condition* for entering the sea of Buddha's teachings, it is said that faith is primary in the Buddhist religion. M. Saigusa, a renowned Japanese expert on the *Ta-chih-tu lun*, comments on the passages cited here as follows:

> In Nāgārjuna, salvation is the function of wisdom whereas faith is the entrance, nothing more than that

(this is also true with other passages in the *ta-chih-tu lun*). This means that Nāgārjuna's position is basically philosophical while discussing religion. That is to say that although faith as that by which one can enter the Buddha's dharma is the indispensably necessary condition, it is not the sufficient condition for Buddhist life.[3]

Thus, according to Saigusa, although faith is primary in the sense of being the "entrance" to the gate of Buddha's teachings, final salvation is ultimately a function of wisdom. However, in other Buddhist texts, a more radical primacy is attributed to faith. For instance, in the *Hua-yen ching*, or *Flower Adornment Scripture*, which is the basic text of the Hua-yen school of Buddhism, a famous passage explicitly declares the primacy of faith:

> Faith is the origin of the Way,
> And the mother of all merit.
> It causes all the roots of goodness to grow;
> It extinguishes all doubts.
> It reveals the Peerless Way,
> And makes it grow.[4]

In the *Hua-yen ching*, the bodhisattva must pass through fifty-two stages of development, beginning with the ten faiths and proceeding to the ten abodes, ten conducts, ten returnings, ten stages (*bhūmi*s), equal enlightenment, and, finally, marvelous enlightenment. This scheme of fifty-two stages is often interpreted by Hua-yen scholars to represent the four aspects of Buddhist religious salvation: faith, understanding, practice, and enlightenment. However, the basic principles of Hua-yen Buddhism are "interpenetration" (*yung-t'ung*) and "nonobstruction" (*wu-ai*) among all phenomena. Every *dharma* contains every other *dharma*, past, present, and future alike. Consequently, all fifty-two stages of a bodhisattva's career interpenetrate without obstruction, so that the first stage of initial faith contains all the other stages, including the fifty-second stage of marvelous enlightenment. Thus, in Hua-yen Buddhism, faith is not only the "origin of the Way," but its culmination as well. It is both the alpha and omega of the bodhisattva's career. Therefore, the Hua-yen school claims a much more radical primacy of faith than does Nāgārjuna, since faith is not only the necessary condition, but also the sufficient condition for salvation. That is, for Hua-yen, salvation is a function of faith, since understanding, practice, and enlightenment are themselves included in the act of faith as its true contents.

Fa-tsang (643–712), the third patriarch of the Hua-yen school, describes the central role of faith in Buddhism in his *Record of Mind's Journey in the Dharma Realm of Hua-yen*:

For those who wish to now enter the unobstructed dharma realm, it is essential first to arouse a resolute faith. Why is it so? Because faith is the primary foundation for all kinds of practices. All practices arise from faith. Therefore, faith is listed first and is made the departure point.[5]

Fa-tsang continues:

If resolute faith is absent, even if there is much understanding, it is only confused thinking. Why is it so? Because understanding without faith does not advance to practice, and confused thinking is not true understanding.[6]

[13]

Here, Fa-tsang explains the basic reason for the primacy of faith in Hua-yen Buddhism: It is because "all practices arise from faith." Faith advances to practice, which in turn produces true understanding and enlightenment. In Buddhism, all religious practices, including *samādhi* ("concentration"), *karuṇā* "(compassion"), and *dāna* ("giving"), arise out of faith as its natural functions. Fa-tsang emphasizes that without faith one remains at the level of intellectual discourse, which leads to confused thinking, and never advances to the levels of practice, understanding and enlightenment. He therefore identifies the act of arousing a resolute faith as the true point of departure in the career of a bodhisattva. Again, however, faith is not only the point of departure; it also sustains the bodhisattva in his vows, acts, and practices in the intermediate stages before he finally attains the fifty-second stage of marvelous enlightenment, which Fa-tsang conceives as the "perfection of faith."

The most important Buddhist text addressing the problem of faith is undoubtedly the *Ta-ch'eng ch'i-hsin lun*, or *Treatise on Awakening Mahāyāna Faith*. This key work has served as a basic text not only for the Hua-yen school, but for virtually the entire East Asian tradition of Mahāyāna Buddhism, including the various Ch'an (Korean: Sŏn; Japanese: Zen), or meditation, sects. The basic theme of this treatise, as implied by the title, is how to arouse a resolute faith and how to perfect this faith through different practices in order to attain perfect enlightenment. The primacy of faith is declared in the Invocation, in which the author explains his reasons for composing the work:

[I] declare that there is a truth which can arouse the root of Mahāyāna faith. Therefore, [I] must explain it

[14]

. . . .[7] because I wish to cause sentient beings to eliminate doubts and forsake wrong attachments, and in order to awaken [in them] right Mahāyāna faith so that the Buddha seed does not perish.[8]

What is "right Mahāyāna faith"? In the earliest Buddhist texts the idea of faith was conveyed by the ancient Sanskrit word *śraddhā*, which is composed of the verbal root *śrat*, "to be trustful, steadfast, confident," or "to have conviction," and *dhā*, "to support, uphold, sustain." Thus, the Buddhist term *śraddhā* denotes the act of sustaining confidence, remaining steadfast, or supporting trust, in the sense of abiding firmly. To convey this sense, Buddhist faith as *śraddhā* is compared to a huge mountain, solid wall, or immovable boulder.

In addition to *śraddhā*, early Buddhist texts also used the Sanskrit terms *prasāda* and *adhimukti* to convey the idea of faith. Whereas *śraddhā* is translated into classical Chinese as *hsin* ("faith") or sometimes *wen-hsin* ("faith by listening"), *prasāda* is translated as *ching-hsin* ("faith by purification") and *adhimukti* as *chieh-hsin* ("faith with understanding"). The word *prasāda* is composed of the Sanskrit prefix *pra* and the verbal root *sad*, "to sink down" or "to sit." Thus, *prasāda* also implies being firmly rooted. The dictionary meaning of *prasāda* is "to grow clear and bright," or "to become placid and tranquil." When all these meanings are taken together, the term *prasāda* can be defined as "being firmly seated in a state of clearness and tranquility." This interpretation of *prasāda* is supported by its Chinese translation as *ching-hsin*, "faith by purification." The Sanskrit word *adhimukti* is composed of the prefix *adhi* and the verbal root *muc*, "to liberate," "to release," or "to be free." As a whole, the word *adhimukti* means "trust" or

[15]

"confidence." When these meanings are combined, one may take *adhimukti* to indicate "abiding with confidence in a state of freedom." In the final analysis, the Buddhist notion of faith as conveyed by the terms *śraddhā*, *prasāda*, and *adhimukti* includes the connotations of practice and enlightenment in the sense of "abiding firmly with resolute conviction in a state of clearness, tranquility, and freedom."⁹

Finally, the primacy of faith operated in the Buddhist soteriological system raises the important issue of the relation between faith and understanding. The relation between faith and understanding was of course one of the most famous controversies of Western Medieval theology. St. Augustine established a tradition based on the primacy of faith, often summarized in the well-known maxim of Anselm: *Credo ut intelligam*, "I believe in order to understand." In the Augustinian tradition, Christianity is described as "faith seeking understanding," so that "philosophy is the handmaiden of theology." Augustine's primacy of faith over understanding is very clearly stated when he writes:

> Faith precedes reason, it cleanses the heart that it may bear the light of greater reason. Therefore, it is reasonably said by the prophet, "Unless you believe, you will not understand" (Is 7:9). In discerning these two, he meant that we may be able to understand that which we believe.¹⁰

For Augustine, then, one cannot understand unless one first awakens faith. However, there is nonetheless a profound interaction between faith and understanding in Augustine's system. This is seen by Augustine's famous definition of faith as "thinking with assent," wherein assent represents the affective and volitional aspects of faith. Augustine explains this cooperation of faith and understanding in one of his sermons:

> From one aspect he is right when he says, "May I understand in order to believe." And I am right when I say with the Prophet, "Believe in order that you may understand." We both speak the truth and agree. Therefore, understand in order that you may believe; believe in order that you may understand. Briefly I explain how we can accept each other's opinion without controversy. Believe God's word in order that you may understand.[11]

This inseparability between faith and understanding described by Augustine at once calls to mind the Hua-yen and Ch'an system of "round-sudden faith and understanding" developed by Chinul, Korea's great 12th-century monk. According to Chinul's system, faith must precede the levels of understanding, practice and enlightenment, as stated by the Hua-yen scheme of fifty-two stages. However, faith and understanding are still regarded as inseparable by Chinul:

> Once right faith is born, it should necessarily be accompanied by understanding. Yung-ming [Yen-shou] says, "Faith without understanding enhances ignorance, and understanding without faith enhances distortion of view." Therefore, you should know that only when faith and understanding are combined can one enter enlightenment.[12]

It must be pointed out, however, that for Chinul, as well as Augustine, the type of understanding established by faith is not only an intellectual understanding, but also a kind of "inward illumination." Augustine's faith is a divine illumination, reflecting a theory of knowledge derived from Neo-Platonism. Christ, God's Incarnated Word, is said to illumine the mind in the light of faith, purifying the heart so that it can bear the light of greater reason. Similarly, Chinul regards the understanding involved in an act of faith as what he terms *panjo* or "inward illumination," whereby one awakens to True Mind. Yet, there are important differences between Chinul's theory of illumination by faith and Augustine's. For Augustine, illumination means seeing eternal truths (e.g., blessedness, goodness, virtue, etc.) in the light of greater reason, while recognizing the source of that light as from God, as well as seeing in the world the reflections of these divine ideas according to which it was made. The light of faith does not give us an immediate knowledge of God according to Augustine. In contrast, Chinul's enlightenment by faith does not involve a theistic system, nor does it involve a theory of eternal ideas, but instead the means to realize directly the nature of our own True Mind. The structure of Chinul's system of enlightenment by faith will be developed in the following chapter.

Chapter Two
Patriarchal Faith and Doctrinal Faith

In Buddhism, the first step in achieving right practice and right enlightenment is to arouse right faith. What is right faith? In the previous chapter it was suggested that right faith means "abiding firmly with resolute conviction in a state of clearness, tranquility, and freedom." However, at this point, we must distinguish between two radically different kinds of Buddhist faith: patriarchal faith (Chinese: *tsu hsin*) and doctrinal faith (*chiao hsin*). Whereas doctrinal faith is the commitment that "I can *become* Buddha," patriarchal faith is the affirmation that "I am *already* Buddha." Therefore, patriarchal faith is not to be regarded as a "preliminary" to enlightenment, as is doctrinal faith, but as equivalent to enlightenment itself. To arouse patriarchal faith is to become instantly enlightened. In his *Direct Explanation of True Mind*, Chinul clearly distinguishes between patriarchal faith and doctrinal faith:

> Question: What is the difference between faith in the patriarchal and doctrinal teachings?
> Answer: There are many differences. The doctrinal teachings encourage people to have faith in the principle of cause and effect . . . . Those who look for the Buddha as an effect [of practice] have faith that the practice of the six *pāramitās* over three *kalpas* is its primary cause, and *bodhi* [wisdom] and *nirvāṇa* are its suitable effect. Patriarchal faith is not the same as

[19]

above, because patriarchs do not depend upon any principle of cause and effect in the conditional world. It only stresses that there be faith that everyone is originally Buddha; that all people intrinsically possess the perfect Buddha nature; and that the marvellous essence of *nirvāṇa* is perfectly complete in everyone. Hence, there is no need to search anywhere else, because since the beginning, those have been complete in oneself.[1]

According to Chinul, realization of Buddhahood in the case of doctrinal faith depends on a *gradual* process of "cause and effect." However, in the case of patriarchal faith there is no cause-and-effect process of gradual cultivation since one simply affirms that "one's self is originally Buddha." Therefore, patriarchal faith results in *sudden enlightenment*. Actually, Chinul derived his notion of patriarchal faith from Li T'ung-hsüan (646–740), a Chinese Hua-yen scholar who was a contemporary of Fa-tsang. Li T'ung-hsüan's great contribution was his emphasis on the primacy of faith. His purpose was to stress the *practicable* aspects of Hua-yen. For Li T'ung-hsüan, faith was the form in which enlightenment became *available* or *accessible* and was thus the door to Buddhahood. Moreover, he transformed the traditional meaning of Buddhist faith as a commitment to the possibility of becoming Buddha through gradual cultivation into the revolutionary idea that faith is the affirmation that one is already Buddha. Li T'ung-hsüan states his position while discussing the doctrine of ten faiths in the Hua-yen system of fifty-two stages:

If anyone in the stage of the ten levels of faith does not believe that his own body is the same as the Buddha body and that there is no distinction between the causal state [gradual practice] and effect [enlightenment], then he has not realized the perfection of faith supported by wisdom.[2]

In the preface to his *Hwaŏmnon Chŏryo,* which is a summary of Li T'ung-hsüan's *Commentary of the Hua-yen Sūtra,* Chinul quotes a similar passage by Li describing the initial awakening of faith in the first of the ten levels of faith outlined by Hua-yen. According to Li, with the initial awakening of faith, the bodhisattva has three realizations:

(1) He is awakened to the fact that his body and mind are originally the *dharmadhātu.* . . . . (2) He is awakened to the truth that his body and mind, and even his faculty of discriminating itself are originally the Buddha of immovable wisdom. (3) He is awakened to the truth that the marvelous wisdom of discriminating right and wrong is none other than Mañjuśrī. At the initial stage of faith, one is awakened to the above three truths.[3]

The radical nature of Li's conception of faith should now be apparent. As soon as one's faith is aroused, one has the sudden realization that one's own body and mind are the Buddha, the wisdom of Mañjuśrī, and the *dharmadhātu,* the Hua-yen *dharma* realm of unobstructed interpenetration. This is the faith that Chinul adopted in his own system and named "patriarchal faith," the affirmation that "I am Buddha."

What roles do doctrinal and patriarchal faith play in the Ch'an (meditation) school founded by first patriarch Bodhidharma? Whereas doctrinal faith is the basis for a system of "gradual enlightenment," as advocated by the Northern school of Ch'an allegedly founded by Shen-hsiu (?–706 A.D.), patriarchal faith is the basis for a system of "sudden enlightenment," as advocated by the Southern school founded by the sixth patriarch Hui-neng (638–713). Through the rigorous efforts of modern scholars, including Hu-shih, Demieville, Sekiguchi, and Yanagida, many critical and probing questions have been raised about the origin of the Ch'an school and its various sects, the historicity of Bodhidharma and his works, Hui-neng and the authorship of the *Platform Sūtra*, and so on. The focus on questions such as these is probably surprising to traditional East Asian Buddhists concerned with Buddhist thought, as well as to members of the Buddhist community itself, for whom the study of Ch'an has been devoted mainly to a single issue: the meaning, on the deepest level, of the doctrines attributed to such persons as Bodhidharma and Hui-neng. Neither of these groups has ever asked whether Bodhidharma really came to China but *why* he came, what his real message was, how he attempted to transmit it, and, most importantly, how one might personally attain full realization of its meaning.

Why did Bodhidharma come to China? In one account, he is recorded as having said, "I came to China not to make people Buddhas, but to tell them they are already perfect Buddhas." The Southern school of Ch'an has traditionally told this story to illustrate the doctrine of sudden enlightenment. It clearly represents a rejection of the doctrinal faith that "I can become Buddha" in favor of the patriarchal faith that "I am already Buddha."

Another difference between patriarchal and doctrinal faith can be found in two verses of the *Platform Sūtra*, one allegedly composed by Shen-hsiu and the other by Hui-neng. These two verses are frequently cited as showing the difference between the gradual and sudden enlightenment of the Northern and Southern schools respectively. Shen-hsiu wrote:

[22]

The body is the Bodhi tree,
The mind is like a mirror bright.
At all times we must strive to polish it,
And not let the dust alight.[4]

Hui-neng wrote:

Bodhi originally has no tree,
The mirror also has no stand.
Buddha nature is always clean and pure,
Where is there room for dust?[5]

Whereas the verse attributed to Shen-hsiu reflects the doctrinal faith that "I can *become* Buddha," that attributed to Hui-neng reflects the patriarchal faith that "I *am* Buddha."

Dōgen (1200-1235), the most renowned Zen master in the history of Japan, provided one of the strongest expressions of patriarchal faith in his *Shōbōgenzō:*

Because it is [produced] not by forcing oneself, by one's contrivance, or by being coerced by others . . . . faith has been transmitted directly through patriarchs in India and China . . . . faith is one with the fruit of enlightenment; the fruit of enlightenment is one with faith. If it is not the fruit of enlightenment, faith is not realized. Therefore, it is said that faith is the entrance to the ocean of Dharma. Indeed where faith is achieved, there is the realization of the buddhas and patriarchs.[6]

Here, Dōgen claims that the achievement of faith is itself the realization of the Buddhas and patriarchs, enlightened individuals who realized their inherent Buddhahood, and that this faith "has been transmitted directly through patriarchs." It is for this reason that faith in one's own identity with Buddha is termed

[23]

"patriarchal faith" by Chinul. In the tradition of these patriarchs, faith assumes a radical character, since the act of arousing faith is considered to have the potency to produce sudden enlightenment.

At this point, we must raise two questions: Is sudden enlightenment possible and, if so, what conditions must be satisfied? I contend that, if sudden enlightenment is indeed possible, it can occur only on the basis of a patriarchal faith; that is, patriarchal faith is itself the condition for achieving immediate awakening. Why is this so? Let us recall the traditional Hua-yen Buddhist structure of ten faiths, ten abodes, ten practices, ten returnings, ten stages, equal enlightenment, and marvelous enlightenment. Clearly, within this structure, if sudden enlightenment is to occur at all, it can occur only at the first stage of initial faith. Therefore, the kind of faith that one has completely determines whether one's enlightenment is gradual or sudden. If one is to achieve sudden enlightenment, one must have a faith which affirms that one is *already* Buddha. For this reason, the stage of initial faith must be the actual *locus* of the occurrence of sudden enlightenment.

Chapter Three
Buddha-nature and
Patriarchal Faith

I have repeatedly defined patriarchal faith as the affirmation that "I am Buddha"; yet we must now ask: What does it mean to proclaim that "I am Buddha"? What is Buddha? The history of Buddhism is, of course, extremely complex, and the meaning of "Buddha" varies widely. Nonetheless, I shall initially define "Buddha" as the reality of "dependent origination" (Sanskrit: *pratītyasamutpāda*; Chinese: *yüan-ch'i*). In the *Majjhima-nikāya* the Buddha is recorded as saying, "Those who see 'dependent origination' will see the *dharma*; those who see the *dharma* will see 'dependent origination.' "[1] In the *Samyutta-nikāya* the Buddha said, "Those who see the *dharma* will see me; those who see me will see the *dharma*."[2] When we combine these two statements, we arrive at the understanding that Buddha is the world of dependent origination, i.e., the way all *dharma*s arise through conditional coproduction. Therefore, "I am Buddha" must also mean "I am dependent origination."

In Hua-yen Buddhism, the key idea of the *dharmadhātu*, or "*dharma* world," is traditionally defined in terms of dependent origination (*pratītyasamutpāda*) as has been demonstrated at great length by the famous Japanese Buddhist scholar H. Ui.[3] Therefore, in Hua-yen terms, to say that "I am Buddha" is to say that "I am one in essence with the *dharmadhātu*." For this reason, Li T'ung-hsüan claims that upon arousing initial faith one realizes that one's body and mind are originally the *dharmadhātu*. In the final analysis, the patriarchal faith which affirms that "I am Buddha" is the realization of the *dharmadhātu* of dependent origination.

In his *Mūlamadhyamakakārikā*, Nāgārjuna defines *pratītyasamutpāda* as *śūnyatā*, or "emptiness": "The 'originating dependently' we call 'emptiness.' "[4] Therefore, implicit in the statement "I am Buddha" is the realization of the emptiness of all things, since they arise by dependent orgination. Patriarchal faith actually involves the awakening of what Buddhism calls *prajñā*, "the wisdom that realizes emptiness and dependent origination." In an initial act of patriarchal faith, one suddenly realizes dependent origination by which all *dharma*s arise as emptiness. It is clear, then, that Buddhist faith is quite different from the faith of theistic religions, for it is not a belief in the truth of scriptures, in the divinity of a Savior, or in the existence of a transcendent God; rather, it is the direct experience of dependent origination, in which all dharmas are empty.

That which makes Buddhist faith a patriarchal faith is the *suddenness* of the realization of emptiness and dependent origination. How is this sudden realization possible? The school of sudden enlightenment usually argues that it is possible because all *dharma*s are originally Buddha, which means that they have arisen through dependent origination. Since all *dharma*s are originally Buddha, sudden enlightenment can occur at any instant. That is, sudden enlightenment is possible because all *dharma*s are ontologically grounded in emptiness.

We can summarize the argument as follows: If Buddha is identical to dependent origination and all *dharma*s arise through dependent origination, then all *dharma*s are originally Buddha. The fact that all *dhar-*

mas are originally Buddha provides the grounds for sudden enlightenment, or the patriarchal faith that "I am Buddha." By this line of reasoning, the position of patriarchal faith seems more logically convincing than that of doctrinal faith, which holds merely that "I can *become* Buddha."

Our definition of patriarchal faith as the realization of dependent origination calls to mind an interesting connection to the Western theology of faith developed by Friedrich Schleiermacher (1768–1834). Schleiermacher defined faith as a "feeling of absolute dependence." In his book called *The Christian Faith*, he states:

> . . . . We spoke above of faith in God, which was nothing but the certainty concerning the feeling of absolute dependence, as such, i.e., as conditioned by a Being placed outside of us, and as expressing our relation to Being.[5]

Schleiermacher's definition of faith as a feeling of absolute dependence is highly suggestive, although in the context of Mahāyāna Buddhist faith, it must undergo a major adjustment. The patriarchal faith of Mahāyāna Buddhism could similarly be defined as a "feeling of absolute dependence," but only in the sense of dependent coorigination or conditioned coproduction, as opposed to the theistic framework of Schleiermacher's theology, wherein dependence means being ontologically supported by an external and transcendent God. Therefore, if we understand the word "dependence" to mean the mutual dependence between all dharmas as described by the Mahāyāna Buddhist notion of *pratītyasamutpāda*, then we can truly define patriarchal faith as a feeling of absolute dependence.

Although we have defined *pratītyasamutpāda* as interdependence, and patriarchal faith as the affirmation that "I am Buddha," in the sense of a feeling of interdependence, we can now extend the discussion in terms of the doctrine of Buddha-nature. In Mahāyāna Buddhism, the doctrine of Buddha-nature explains the possibility of not only universal enlightenment, but even sudden enlightenment. According to this theory, since sentient beings have an indwelling Buddha-nature, they can realize instant enlightenment at any given moment. However, before Tao-sheng (died 433 A.D.), the famous *Nirvāṇa-sūtra* scholar, boldly insisted that everyone has Buddha-nature, the idea was not welcomed by people. Thus, some monks branded this idea as being heretical and wanted to expel him from the order. Nonetheless, Tao-sheng was so firm in his position as to proclaim that all sentient beings possess Buddha-nature, and that all are capable of attaining Buddhahood through sudden enlightenment. Fortunately for Tao-sheng, soon afterward the celebrated translator Dharmakshema translated a more completed form of the *Nirvāṇa-sūtra* entitled *Ta-p'in nieh-pan-ching*, which clearly states that all living beings have inherent Buddha-nature and are capable of achieving enlightenment. The monks who accused Tao-sheng were thereby shamed by this, and forced to admire Tao-sheng's insights.[6]

However, this was by no means the end of the debate about Buddha-nature among early Chinese scholars. Although various doctrinal interpretations of Buddha-nature were given by the different schools, the debate can be narrowed down to two fundamentally different theories:

1. Buddha-nature is universally possessed by all sentient beings;
2. some classes of sentient beings do not have Buddha-nature.

Whereas the first theory was advocated by Tao-sheng and his followers, the second theory was initiated by Hsüan-tsang's Fa-hsiang school. Hsüan-tsang's successor K'uei-chi (632–682) openly stated that the term "everyone" in the sentence "everyone has Buddha-nature" in the *Nirvāṇa-sūtra* does not mean "everyone without exception", but instead means only "almost everyone." In this way, K'uei-chi supported the "five ranks" doctrine of human nature, which holds that the fifth rank of people are devoid of Buddha-nature, and thus, incapable of realizing Buddhahood. Later, Fa-tsang of the Hua-yen school harmonized the dispute by arguing that both Tao-sheng and K'uei-chi see only one aspect of suchness: In terms of initial teaching, five ranks of human beings are recognized in the scriptures, whereas in terms of final teaching, the scriptures teach only one nature in human beings, namely, the Buddha-nature.[7]

Daijō Tokiwa, a renowned Buddhist scholar on the Buddha-nature, describes Fa-tsang's contribution to the debate of Buddha-nature, which we can summarize as follows: It should be noted in Fa-tsang's theory that (1) the two aspects of Buddha-nature, i.e., universal aspect in principle, and particular aspect in practice, are dependently cooriginated; (2) the differences seen in human beings are not because of different human nature but because of different stages in practice; and (3) therefore, practitioners are supposed to perform a transformation of stages.[8] It is clear that Fa-tsang's solution is derived from his theory of *tathāgatagarbha-pratītyasamutpāda*, which he borrowed from the Suchness/arising-ceasing aspects of One Mind described in the *Treatise on Awakening Mahāyāna Faith*. According to Jikidō Takasaki's remarkable research on *Tathāgatagarbha* thought, the notion of *tathāgatagarbha* or "womb of Tathāgata" is synonymous with Buddha-nature.[9] As the term suggests, *tathāgatagarbha* means that there is a cause in sentient beings to become Tathāgata. It is interesting to note that the passage "All sentient beings have Buddha-nature" found in the *Nirvāṇa-sūtra* and the passage, "All sentient beings have *tathāgatagarbha*" found in the *Ratnagotravibhāga* are identical in terms of their soteriological message. The *Ratnagotravibhāga* says:

> Since the wisdom of Buddha is penetrated into sentient beings;
> since they are originally not different in the purified forms;
> since in the Buddha-nature its effect is assumed,
> it is said that all sentient beings have the embryo of Buddha[10]

Thus, it can be argued that the doctrines of Buddha-nature and *tathāgatagarbha-pratītyasamutpāda*, whereby all sentient beings without exception are endowed with embryonic Buddhahood, provide us with a profound basis for the theory of patriarchal faith and its related notion of sudden enlightenment. However, we can further extend our discussion of Buddha-nature by considering it under three aspects, namely, the so-called *trikāya* or "triple body" theory of Buddha. Originally, the word "Buddha" simply meant an Enlightened One. It was only one of ten epithets given to Gautama Siddhartha after he awakened to the Truth. It is well known that Buddha admonished his disciples not to deify him. Nevertheless, the *Lotus Sūtra* emphasizes that Buddha's body is everlasting. Here Buddha is thought of as having two bodies: (1) the flesh body or *rūpakāya* which is impermanent, and (2) the truth body or *dharmakāya* which is everlasting. However, scholars then met a difficulty in combining *rūpa-kāya* with *dharma-kāya*, and for this reason introduced a third body, i.e., *sambhoga-kāya* or the "enjoyment body," which is the body of thirty-two marks attained by Buddha through *kalpas* of practice and holding vows.

In the tradition of Yogācāra, the triple body theory of Buddha includes *svābhāvika-kāya* or essence body, *sāmbhogika-kāya* or enjoyment body, and *nairmāṇika-kāya* or transformation body. Here *svābhāvikāya* and *nairmāṇika-kāya* correspond to the traditional notions of *dharmakāya* and *rūpakāya*. The Yogācāra school's contribution to the subject is to be seen in their explanation of *sambhogika-kāya* or enjoyment body. According to Yogācāra, the enjoyment body has two aspects. The first aspect is the enjoyment of Gautama Buddha himself such as his enjoyment of enlightenment under the *bodhi* tree, whereas the second aspect is the enjoyment of others listening to Gautama's sermons. Therefore, as far as our appreciation of Buddha is concerned, his aspect as *sambhogika-kāya* is the most important. From the standpoint of sentient beings, *dharmakāya* is too abstract and remote, although it is universal and basic in the sense that every conception of Buddha is grounded in his *dharmakāya* aspect, which is his aspect as *śūnyatā* or emptiness. Moreover, in his *rūpakāya* or flesh body aspect, Buddha seems too ordinary and impermanent. However, *sambhogika-kāya* or the enjoyment body of Buddha has both the truth body aspect and flesh body aspect. Now our question is how these three bodies are interrelated through the enjoyment body.[11]

In his well-known paper entitled, "On the Theory of Buddha-Body," Gadjin Nagao states:

Thus, we know that the Sāmbhogika-kāya is composed of a twofold character. While, on the one hand, there is the aspect of transcending the human Buddha, the nairmāṇika-kāya, there is, on the other hand, the concretization of the absolute, the svābhākika-kāya. Therefore, the sāmbhogika-kāya has the two aspects of being at once transcending and phenomenal, and at once historic and super-historic. When the historic Buddha is contrasted with the super-historic Body, it is commonly done in the light of the two-body theory, signifying the Physical-body and the Dharma-body. Contrary to this, the sāmbhogika-kāya, while modelling itself after the historic Buddha, is a temporal and spatial presentation of the absolure dharma-nature. The story of Amida Buddha as the Reward-body is not something like a myth of a stage before history; even if we might call it a myth, it was produced by the association of history with super-history. It is due to this character of the sāmbhogika-kāya that such things as the thirty-two physical marks of the Buddha are attributed to the sāmbhogika-kāya, and the buddhaland as the Pure Land is exclusively told in connection with the sāmbhogika-kāya.

Nagao continues:

The Enjoyment body, through this double character, lies between the Essence Body and the Transformation Body, serving as a link between the two. No, the Enjoyment Body rather occupies the control position in the triple-body doctrine; especially, the soteriology in Buddhism is developed revolving around the axis of this double character of the Enjoyment Body. In this sense, the Enjoyment Body should be considered as the real Buddha-body.[12]

In the above, Nagao states that the Enjoyment Body cannot be thought of apart from Gautama Buddha's enlightenment experience and his sermon which causes people to share in his enjoyment. We find this same point expressed in Sthirmati's definition of the enjoyment body, stating: "The enjoyment body just refers to the state of essence body which realizes enlightenment."[13]

Nagao compares the difference between the essence body and the enjoyment body to that of original enlightenment and actualization of enlightenment discussed in the *Treatise on Awakening Mahāyāna Faith*, in which original enlightenment is described as one's inherent Buddha-nature amidst defilement whereas the actualization of enlightenment is the enlightenment once defilement is removed. The key issue in this section of the *Treatise on Awakening Mahāyāna Faith* is that original enlightenment and actualization of enlightenment are not different. Hence, according to this reasoning, the essence body and the enjoyment body of Buddha should also not be different.[14]

However, what is available at the level of sentient beings is the enjoyment body, through which we are able to see the essence body of Buddha. Here the difficulty lies in the fact that the enjoyment body and the transformation body seem alike to sentient beings. To ordinary people, the enjoyment body is seen as the transformation body. Therefore, the Buddhist practitioner must strive to see the enjoyment body in the transformation body. To see the enjoyment body means to see the essence body in the transformation body. Thus, it might be said that to see the enjoyment body is the key to all the Buddha-bodies.

To see the essence body in the transformation body through the enjoyment body can be comparable to the Christian's effort of seeing God the Father in Jesus. According to the *Gospel of John*, Jesus said:

> "If you knew me you would know my father too. From now on you do know him; you have seen him," Philip said to him, "Lord, show us the Father and we ask no more." Jesus answered, "Have I been with you

[33]

so long, and yet you do now know me Philip? He who
has seen me has seen the Father; how can you say
'show us the Father'? Do you not believe that I am in
the Father and the Father in me? . . . . Believe me that
I am in the Father and the Father in me."[15]

In his book entitled, *Buddha and the Gospel of Buddhism,* A. K. Coomaraswamy says that the essence
body, enjoyment body and transformation body of
Buddha correspond respectively to the Father, the
figure of Christ in Glory, and the visible Jesus. It might
be said that whereas the Christian must learn to see
God the Father in Jesus through Christ in Glory, the
Buddhist must learn to see the essence body in the
transformation body through the enjoyment body. Of
course, we can carry the analogy only so far here, since
Christianity restricts Godhood only to Jesus, whereas
Buddhism attributes Buddhahood not only to
Gautama Siddhartha, but to all sentient beings equally.

How can one learn to see the essence body in the
transformation body through the enjoyment body? In
Buddhism, the answer lies in the arousing of a patriarchal faith, which affirms not only my own Buddhahood, but the Buddhahood of everyone. Here
"Buddha" represents the essence body whereas "I"
represents the transformation body. By connecting "I"
with "Buddha" through the copula "am," the sentence
"I am Buddha" represents the enjoyment body. It can
thus be said that the arousal of a patriarchal faith indicates that one has awakened to the essence body in
the transformation body through the mediation of an
enjoyment body. Therefore, awakening patriarchal
faith means the ability to see the unenlightened as the
enlightened, or to see ordinary people as Buddha, including oneself.

Chapter Four
Essence-Function Versus
Subject-Object Constructions

Since doctrinal faith affirms only that "I can become Buddha," it claims a distance between myself and Buddha, so that Buddha becomes an object of faith and worship. Thus, Buddhist faith is commonly expressed erroneously in terms of a dualistic "subject-object" or "faith in ———" construction such as "I believe in Buddha." In Western theism, this takes the form of "I believe in God" or "I believe in Jesus Christ." Generally speaking, the dualistic "faith in ———" construction is what is meant by "doctrinal faith." The *neng-so*, or "subject-object," structure of doctrinal faith dominates the life of all sentient beings in *saṃsāra* or transmigration, not only in the case of the six sense organs and their six sense fields, but also in the case of creator and creature, birth and death, cause and effect, arising and ceasing, and all other dichotomies. As long as people are attached to the dualistic *neng-so* construction, they are prevented from seeing that they themselves are already perfect Buddhas and therefore seek Buddha outside themselves, believing only that they have the potential to become a Buddha.[1]

However, in the case of patriarchal faith there is no objectification of Buddha. Iconoclastic tendencies cultivated in Ch'an monasteries, as expressed in Lin-chi's famous utterance "If you meet Buddha, kill him; and also when you meet patriarchs, kill them!" can be interpreted as reflecting patriarchal faith.[2] Patriarchal faith has no object. Patriarchal faith is not a faith *in* the patriarchs; it is the faith *of* the patriarchs. Instead of the dualistic *neng-so*, or "subject-object," construction of doctrinal faith, the basic hermeneutic device of patriarchal faith is the nondual *t'i-yung*, or "essence-function," construction. In the hermeneutic traditions of East Asia, *t'i*, or "essence," refers to the noumenal, internal, and invisible aspects of reality, whereas *yung*, or "function," refers to its phenomenal, external, and visible aspects. The purpose of the *t'i-yung* formula is to show the inseparability of two seemingly separate but in reality nondistinct things.[3] One of the earliest classical works of Ch'an literature in China, the *Platform Sūtra*, illustrated the relation between *t'i* and *yung* with the analogy of a lamp and its light. Whereas the bright lamp is *t'i*, "essence," its light is *yung*, "function," so that a candle and its light are inseparable and nondual.[4] Thus, the purpose of the *t'i-yung* hermeneutic device in Chinese Buddhist texts is to remove false discrimination originating from a dualistic way of thinking, as reflected in such dichotomies as subject-object, means-end, cause-effect, arising-cessation, and birth-death.

Since *t'i* represents the noumenal, internal, and invisible aspect of reality and *yung* represents its phenomenal, external, and visible aspects, ordinary sentient beings can usually see only the *yung* aspects of phenomena, whereas only enlightened Buddhas are able to see its *t'i* aspects. Consequently, sentient beings should not be overwhelmed by the Buddha's acts (*yung*) but must also discern the Buddha's wisdom (*t'i*); otherwise, they might reduce these acts to their own level. A Buddhist must focus on the hidden *t'i* aspect insofar as Buddhist practice does not consist simply of imitating the Buddha's acts, but also of realizing their inner essence. As soon as the *t'i* of an act is present, the *yung* simultaneously appears.

It should now be clear that the *neng-so* or "subject-object" understanding of Buddhist faith as represented by doctrinal faith and the *t'i-yung*, or "essence-function," understanding of Buddhist faith as represented by patriarchal faith are radically different. Whereas in the case of doctrinal faith, Buddha is the object of one's faith, in the case of patriarchal faith, Buddha, who is actually the Mind of sentient beings, represents *t'i* and faith is its active *yung*.

The *t'i-yung* construction of patriarchal faith was developed with great clarity by Wŏnhyo (617-686), the eminent Korean Buddhist scholar and saint of the Unified Silla dynasty.[5] Wŏnhyo's *Kishillonso*, or *Commentary on Awakening Mahāyāna Faith*, also called the *Haedongso* by the Chinese (an honorific title meaning *The Korean Commentary*), is one of the three most authoritative expositions on the *Ta-ch'eng chi'-hsin lun*, or *Treatise on Awakening Mahāyāna Faith*, the other two having been written by Fa-tsang (643-712), the famous third patriarch of Chinese Hua-yen Buddhism, and Hui-yüan (523-592).[6] In his commentary Wŏnhyo argues that the *Ta-ch'eng ch'i-hsin lun* was originally a nonsectarian text revealing a hermeneutic principle by which to achieve a "harmonization of all disputes" (*hwajaeng*) and a "Buddhism of total interpenetration" (*t'ong pulgyo*), namely, the *t'i-yung*, or "essence-function," formula described above. Therefore, Wŏnhyo applies the *t'i-yung* construction to all of the central concepts in the *Ta-ch'eng ch'i-hsin lun* in order to reveal their deeper meanings. For instance, he skillfully applies the *t'i-yung* formula to the first line of the Invocation concerning the relationship between the acts and wisdom of Buddha. As mentioned previously wisdom is *t'i*, whereas acts are *yung*. In the case of the Buddha, compassionate acts are the external function of his inner wisdom such that the two are indivisible.[7]

Wŏnhyo also uses the *t'i-yung* formula as a

hermeneutic device for interpreting the meaning of the title of the text itself. In the tradition of East Asian commentary, the correct interpretation of a text's title has special significance for revealing the essence of the text's meaning. Thus, Wŏnhyo's insights into the title of the *Ta-ch'eng ch'i-hsin lun* provide a key not only to the understanding of patriarchal faith, but also to the essence of the entire work. If one translates *Ta-ch'eng ch'i'hsin lun* as *Treatise on the Awakening of Faith in Mahāyāna*, as has been done by all translators without exception, the term *ta-ch'eng*, or "Mahāyāna," becomes the object of *ch'i-hsin*, or "awakening faith," thus establishing a *neng-so*, or "subject–object," structure wholly alien to the text and to Mahāyāna Buddhism in general. According to Wŏnhyo, *ta-ch'eng* is not the object of *ch'i-hsin*. Rather, "Mahāyāna," meaning "great carrier" or "great vehicle," i.e., One Mind or "the Mind of sentient beings," represents *t'i*, or "internal essence," whereas faith represents *yung*, or "external function." In Wŏnhyo's words:

> To conclude: Mahāyāna is the essence of the doctrine of this treatise; "awakening faith" is its efficacious function. [Thus], the title is composed [in such a way as] to show the unity of essence and function. Hence the words, "Treatise on Awakening Mahāyāna Faith."[8]

In this way, Wŏnhyo dispenses with the subject-object or "faith in ———" construction and replaces it with the *t'i-yung*, or "essence–function," hermeneutic device. Faith, in its deepest sense as patriarchal faith, is simply the function (*yung*) of One Mind. Therefore, the title of the text now reads *Awakening Mahāyāna Faith* and in the final analysis, comes to mean simply "the naturally functioning mind" or "the properly operating mind," which, in effect, is the "mind of faith."

Our criteria for judging the correctness of the translation of *Ta-ch'eng ch'i-hsin* as *Awakening Mahāyāna Faith* instead of *Awakening of Faith in Mahāyāna* should be those established internally within the text itself. Let us begin by noting that in classical Chinese a verb rarely follows its object except in poetry, in which case rules of grammar are often neglected. Therefore, the most likely relationship between *ta-ch'eng* and *ch'i-hsin* is not that of a verbal phrase (*ch'i-hsin*) and its object (*ta-ch'eng*) but rather that of a qualifier (*ta-ch'eng*) and that which it qualifies (*ch'i-hsin*). This gives strong support to the translation of the title as *Treatise on Awakening Mahāyāna Faith*. The last line of the Invocation — *ch'i ta-ch'eng cheng-hsin*, "awakening right Mahāyāna faith" — and the line following it — *yu fa neng-ch'i mo-ho-yen hsin-ken*, "There is a *dharma* which can arouse the root of Mahāyāna faith"[9] — also support this translation. In these two lines the term "Mahāyāna" functions grammatically simply to qualify "faith"; it is thus highly improbable that "Mahāyāna" in the title is to be taken as the object of "faith." In fact, of the fifty-four occurrences of the term *hsin*, or "faith," in the treatise, it is used as a transitive verb requiring an object only twelve times; in every other instance it is used as a noun obviously not requiring an object.[10]

The following renditions of the two lines in question are taken from five English translations of the *Ta-ch'eng ch'i-hsin lun* (in all cases, italics mine):

D. T. Suzuki:
"by the awakening of faith"
"For the purpose of awakening . . . . a pure *faith in the Mahāyāna*"[11]

Timothy Richards:
"get *Faith in the Great School*"
(no translation)[12]

Wei Tao:
"by the Awakening of their *Faith in the Mahāyāna*"
there is a way in which faith in the Mahāyāna can
be developed"[13]

The Shrine of Wisdom:
"And *faith in Mahāyāna* cause the Soul"[14]
(no translation)

Y. Hakeda:
"to give rise to the correct *faith in Mahāyāna*"
"There is a teaching (dharma) which can awaken in us
the root of faith"[15]

R. Robinson:
"to awaken true *faith in the Mahāyāna*"
"There is a dharma that can arouse the roots of faith in '
the Mahāyāna"[16]

Thus, it has become standard to translate the key
passages referring to faith in the treatise in such a way
that *ta-ch'eng*, or "Mahāyāna," is always an object of
hsin, or "faith." Some scholars might defend these
translations on the grounds that the phrase "awakening
faith in Mahāyāna" does not imply a dualistic "faith in
————" construction in which Mahāyāna (One Mind
or Suchness) is an object of "awakening faith," but instead refers only to the awakening of faith within the
Mahāyāna *tradition*. However, we need only refer to
Y. S. Hakeda's commentary accompanying his translation of the treatise, in which he specifically states that
the term "Mahāyāna" indicates a metaphysical Absolute:

It should be noted that the term "Mahāyāna" here is
not used in the usual sense of the word, that is, Mahā-

yāna versus Hīnayāna. According to the definition given in the discussion immediately following, Mahāyāna designates Suchness or the Absolute. The title of the text, the *Awakening of Faith in the Mahāyāna*, should therefore be understood as the "Awakening of Faith in the Absolute," not in Mahāyāna Buddhism as distinguished from Hīnayāna Buddhism.[17]

Clearly, then, the translation of the title of the treatise as *The Awakening of Faith in Mahāyāna*, reflects the dualistic *neng-so* formula as expressed in the "faith in ————" construction. This, in turn, gives rise to a seriously misleading interpretation of Mahāyāna Buddhism in general and Mahāyāna faith in particular. For this reason, it is especially important to adopt the *t'i-yung* principle introduced in the text itself as the proper basis for understanding Mahāyāna Buddhist faith, whereby the act of arousing faith is now conceived of as the natural *yung*, "function," of One Mind, the Great Vehicle (Mahāyāna), which is known as *t'i*, or "essence."

Having analyzed the *t'i-yung* structure of Buddhist faith, we are now in a position to compare patriarchal and doctrinal faith from another perspective. As was pointed out, the basic purpose of the Buddhist essence-function construction is to establish a framework of nondualism in which no object is required for an act of faith, as is the case with the dualistic *neng-so* construction of faith in theistic religions. Thus, the Buddhist essence-function structure provides a challenging alternative to the theistic "faith in _____" construction. Therefore, the notion of doctrinal faith, or the conviction that "I can *become* Buddha," merely reintroduces the dualistic subject-object structure in different terms. An act of doctrinal faith is separate from its object which is Buddha; i.e., Buddha is posited as the object of one's faith.

[41]

Thus, a dualistic gap is established between "I" and "Buddha," and can be bridged only through gradual cultivation. This, I contend, violates the fundamental nondualistic framework of Buddhist philosophy as expressed by the essence-function construction. If doctrinal faith merely reintroduces the subject-object structure in different terms, then it is simply an extension of our usual dualistic way of thinking, which separates sentient beings from Buddha and delays our salvation. Therefore, the concept of doctrinal faith seems to run counter to Mahāyāna Buddhism, which teaches the identity of sentient beings and Buddha as well as of *saṃsāra* and *nirvāṇa*.

It would take a much more rigorous critical inquiry to determine the validity of the Mahāyāna Buddhist *t'i-yung* principle. Nonetheless, it is my intention to point out at least the internal inconsistency between the idea of doctrinal faith and the nondual framework that characterizes the Buddhist way of thinking.

Chapter Five
Nonbacksliding Faith and Backsliding Faith

In the Invocation of the *Treatise on Awakening Mahāyāna Faith* the author states his basic reason for composing the text: "to eliminate [all] doubts and awaken right Mahāyāna faith." What does "right Mahāyāna faith" mean here? According to the treatise, the criterion for right faith is that it be "non-backsliding" or "unretrogressive" (*pu-t'ui*). The central problem addressed by the treatise is how to transform *t'ui hsin*, the "retrogressive faith," of *aniyata rāśi* (Chinese: *pu-ting chü*), or the "undetermined class," into *pu-t'ui hsin*, the "unretrogressive faith," of *niyata rāśi* (Chinese: *cheng-ting chü*), or the "determined class." In other terms, the problem is to transform *hsin-hsin* (Sanskrit: *śraddhā*), i.e., the "mind of faith," into *fa-hsin* (Sanskrit: *citta utpāda*), i.e., "*bodhi*-mind" or the "mind of wisdom," which means *anuttara samyak sambodhi*, "unexcelled perfect enlightenment." If one's *gotra*, or "family," is *aniyata rāśi*, one has *hsin-hsin*, in which case backsliding is always possible since one's resolve or will is always capable of retrogression. However, if through *āśraya parāvṛtti*, or a "transformation of the basis," one undergoes a complete change from the undetermined class to the determined class, then one comes to have *fa-hsin*, which is incapable of any degree of backsliding or retrogression whatever. This means that a bodhisattva who has achieved a nonbacksliding faith always remains firm in his practice, vows, and holding of precepts.

Whereas those who have doctrinal faith belong to the undetermined class, which is characterized by *t'ui-hsin*, or "backsliding faith," those who have patriarchal faith, belong to the determined class, which is characterized by *pu-t'ui hsin* or "nonbacksliding faith." Those who have transformed *hsin-hsin*, "the mind of faith," into *fa-hsin*, "the mind of wisdom," have fully perfected their faith such that it has become the enlightenment of Buddhahood and have no fear of backsliding into unenlightened existence. So it is written in the *Treatise on Awakening Mahāyāna Faith*:

> Those who are able to realize the mind of wisdom through the perfection of faith will be transformed into *niyata rāśi* or the determined class and will finally never have backsliding.[1]

Clearly, then, the criterion for right faith in this treatise is *pu-t'ui hsin*. However, from the conventional Buddhist perspective, especially the gradual tradition of doctrinal faith, a truly nonbacksliding or unretrogressive faith is not possible. Why is this so? From the gradual point of view, faith is a function of will and intellect. Consequently, since the human intellect can assent to falsehoods and the human will is fallible, it is always possible to backslide; belief can turn to doubt, resolve can weaken, vows and precepts can be broken.

I would argue, however, that patriarchal faith is not a function of will and reason, or, as they are technically called in Christianity, *fiducio* (trust) and *assensus* (intellectual assent).[2] Doctrinal faith is indeed a function of will and reason and, since reason and will are fallible, it can always weaken. Thus, there can be no

[44]

guarantee against retrogression. In contrast, patriarchal faith is not a function of reason and will but of Suchness (Sanskrit: *tathatā*; Chinese: *chen-ju*) in the sense of *pratītyasamautpāda*, "dependent origination," and *śūnyatā*, "emptiness." The immovability and irreversibility of patriarchal faith are derived from the fact that one is *ontologically grounded* in Suchness or dependent origination.

In other terms, patriarchal faith can be understood as a function of One Mind, i.e., the mind of non-discrimination and nonthought. As soon as one returns to One Mind, one no longer discriminates between sentient beings and Buddhas or between enlightenment and nonenlightenment, but instead directly cognizes the world of emptiness and dependent origination. Backsliding is not possible in a mind free of discriminating thoughts. Since no distinctions are made, there is nowhere to backslide to and no one to backslide. Thus, since patriarchal faith is ontologically grounded in dependent origination as a function of One Mind, it is not subject to backsliding in any way whatever.

In the Christian theology of the Protestant reformers Luther and Calvin, faith is considered a gift of God's almighty grace and therefore unobtainable by human effort. Thus, one's intellectual assent and willful resolve are always capable of backsliding. The Protestant idea of faith as a gift of God's grace would be classified in Buddhism as a form of "other-power" (Japanese: *tariki*), since salvation is completely dependent on an external source; yet, as argued earlier, the Christian theistic position presupposes a dualistic subject–object framework expressed by a "faith in ———" construction, in which God is regarded as the object of worship and faith. However, in the nondual *t'i-yung*, or "essence-function," construction presupposed by

Buddhism, especially Ch'an and Hua-yen Buddhism, faith is understood to be a natural function of one's own Mind. Faith is neither derived from nor directed toward an external source. Thus, patriarchal faith is a product of pure "self-power" (*jiriki*) and therefore is not subject to backsliding as is a theistic faith dependent on an external source through pure "other-power."[3]

In order to understand the nonbacksliding nature of patriarchal faith, it is necessary to analyze the concept of *āśraya parāvṛtti*, or "transformation of the basis." The main theme of the *Treatise on Awakening Mahāyāna Faith* is the means of one's faith; yet, according to this treatise, as soon as faith is fully matured and perfected, technically speaking it is no longer "faith." It is thus called *fa-hsin*, which, again, refers to "*bodhi*-mind" or the "mind of wisdom," i.e., *annuttara samyak sambodhi*, "unexcelled perfect enlightenment." Consequently, the mind of faith (*hsin-hsin*) and the mind of wisdom (*fa-hsin*) are two different things. According to this view, the way from the mind of faith to *bodhi*-mind is always open, whereas the way from *bodhi*-mind to the mind of faith is closed. In other words, once someone has entered the land of *bodhi*-mind, he cannot retrogress to the stage of faith. This is termed *pu-t'ui hsin*, or "nonbacksliding faith"; it might also be called an *irreversible* faith. Hence, the transformation from faith to *bodhi*-mind is called a metamorphosis, i.e., *āśraya parāvṛtti*. Once the total "revolution of the basis" has taken place, backsliding is impossible. One's enlightenment cannot be lost, for the perfection of faith means being "reborn" as a Buddha, and a Buddha cannot fall back into the state of an unenlightened sentient being anymore than a baby can "fall back" into the mother's womb, a frog into a tadpole, a flower into a seed, or a butterfly into a caterpillar. Therefore, the difference between *fa-hsin*, "the mind of wisdom," which is the nonbacksliding state of patriarchal faith, and *hsin-hsin*, "the mind of faith," which is the backsliding state of doctrinal faith, is qualitative and not merely one of degree.[4]

What is the main difference between *hsin-hsin* and *fa-hsin?* In order to answer this question, let us ask why in the Old Testament Abraham is considered in the Christian tradition to be the father of faith. Is it not because he was able to give up his only son Isaac, whom he had received when he was over 100 years of age?[5] Similarly, in Buddhism, *dāna*, or "giving without attachment," is frequently emphasized as a practice of faith. Giving others what one has in surplus is not true *dāna* even giving away one's only possession is not *dāna* if it does not jeopardize the foundation of one's life. What is the *dāna* which enables one to have patriarchal faith? What is the most important thing one can give away without attachment? Is it life? No! There is something even more important than life to one who is practicing faith. It is one's faith! It is one's faith itself that is to be given away. The very moment one gives away one's faith, one's own mind becomes Buddha Mind. When one has faith (*hsin-hsin*), one is always liable to fall back; but when one attains *bodhi*-mind through *āśraya parāvṛtti*, or "revolution of the basis," there is no faith at all, so how can backsliding occur? Once one is completely reborn as Buddha through revolution of the basis, one realizes the nonbacksliding faith of *niyata rāśi*, "the determined class," which is simply the patriarchal faith that "I am Buddha."

It can now be seen why, from the Buddhist perspective, it is crucial to argue for a nonbacksliding stage of faith. Since nonbacksliding faith is equivalent to the state of *bodhi*-mind, which is *anuttara samyak sambodhi*, "unexcelled perfect enlightenment," to deny the possibility of nonbacksliding faith is also to deny the possibility of enlightenment and the achievement of Buddhahood. In response to the objection that faith is a function of the fallible human faculties of will and reason and therefore always subject to backsliding, I have argued that this applies only to doctrinal faith, the affirmation that one can become Buddha through the personal effort of gradual practice. However, patriarchal faith is grounded not in reason and will, but in Suchness and dependent origination as a function of One Mind and is therefore not subject to backsliding. Moreover, since the shift from the mind of faith to the mind of wisdom involves an *irreversible* transformation of the basis resulting in a qualitative change, an enlightened Buddha cannot fall back to the state of an unenlightened sentient being. The key to this argument is that patriarchal faith is not a preliminary to enlightenment; it *is* enlightenment. It is this radical equation of faith with enlightenment that allows us to argue for the existence of a true non-backsliding and unretrogressive faith, which is attained by members of the determined class.

Chapter Six
The Two Truths and Skill-in-Means

I have argued here that there is a primacy of faith in Buddhism, since right practice and right enlightenment depend on the arousal of right faith. However, there are two basic kinds of Buddhist faith: doctrinal faith and patriarchal faith. I have argued that patriarchal faith is much more radical and effective than doctrinal faith, since it is the basis for sudden enlightenment; yet, in traditional Buddhist literature, there are many passages that seem to support both doctrinal and patriarchal faith. How can this be explained? I would suggest that doctrinal faith and patriarchal faith, or, as it were, secondary and primary faith, correspond to the well-known "two truths' of Mahāyāna Buddhism: *samvṛti satya* and *paramārtha satya*, "relative truth" and "absolute truth." All enlightened Buddhas attempt to convey their experience through these two truths. Their reference to two different truths does not mean that they have two different kinds of experience but simply that their listeners vary greatly in their degree of receptivity or capacity to understand the Buddhadharma.[1]

Usually, whenever the theory of the two truths is discussed, Nāgārjuna's verses in the chapter of his *Madhyamakakārikā* relating to the four noble truths (XXIV) are cited:

By the two truths
Buddha's teachings are given:

Saṁvṛti satya and *paramārtha satya.*
Those who do not know the difference
Of these two truths
Do not know the deep truths of Buddhism.
Without depending upon the *saṁvṛti satya,*
The *paramārtha satya* cannot be expressed.
Without knowing the *paramārtha satya,*
No one enters *nirvāṇa.*[2]

Although interpretations of the theory of two truths vary, its message is quite clear: the truth was taught by the Buddha himself, in two ways for the sake of sentient beings. In other words, the truth itself cannot be two, but because people's capacities to understand it differ, it is expressed in two ways: the relative way and the absolute way, or the conventional way and the ultimate way. Stated succinctly the theory of two truths, especially Nāgārjuna's version, is a kind of teaching technique or pedagogical device. Relative truth is the truth accepted by ordinary people in the mundane world on the basis of their common sense, whereas the truth accepted by Buddhists, which emphasizes the concepts of emptiness (*śūnyatā*) and no-self (*anātman*), is said to be the absolute truth. Therefore, the truth that is valid in the world of enlightened people is called ultimate or absolute, whereas that which is valid only in the unenlightened world is called relative or conventional. Similarly, it may be said that all effable truths are relative, whereas all ineffable truths are absolute.

Thus, whereas *saṁvṛti satya,* "relative truth," may be said to correspond to doctrinal or secondary faith, which affirms that "I can become Buddha," *paramārtha satya,* "absolute truth," may be said to correspond to nonbacksliding patriarchal faith or primary faith, which affirms that "I am Buddha." From the perspective of Mahāyāna Buddhism, *saṁvṛti satya* and doctrinal faith are justified by the concept of *upāya*, or "skill-in-means," according to which all Buddhist theories and practices are pedagogical tools or expedient devices that must be adjusted to the level of people's receptivity. The *locus classicus* of the doctrine of *upāya* is the famous second chapter of the *Lotus Sūtra*, which states that one should not be attached to the *upāya*s of Buddha because the historical circumstances under which he used them were unique, nor should one blame Buddha for resorting to their use, since it was inevitable. This is illustrated in the text by an analogy: Many small children are playing in a house, which catches on fire. The children's father manages to rescue them, but only by telling them a lie, saying that wagons drawn by animals are waiting for them outside. "Neither attach to the *upāya* or blame the *upāya*" is a famous Mahāyāna proverb.[3]

In view of this theory of *upāya*, there are basically two ways of interpreting the scriptures related to the Buddhist experience of enlightenment: either from the perspective of enlightenment or from the perspective of nonenlightenment. In the first case, the scriptures are assumed to have been written directly for the sake of revealing enlightenment without regard for the level of understanding and receptivity of those attending Buddha's discourse. In the second case, they are considered to have been written for pedagogical purposes, every word having been carefully selected and arranged according to the listeners' levels of understanding so that the listeners might be led to the world of enlightenment. Thus, in the first case, the listeners are assumed to be at Buddha's level, whereas, in the second, the listeners' differing capacities are taken into consideration.

It is claimed by Hua-yen masters that only the *Hua-yen Sūtra* belongs to the first category of scriptures. Thus, according to legend, when the Buddha expounded the *Hua-yen Sūtra*, which describes the *dharma* world of interpenetration, 3,000 of the people in attendance rejected his words and left.[4] Legend can be no more than legend; but we cannot ignore the intention of those who have passed this legend on for several millennia. It is interesting that the Ch'an tradition in China classified the *Hua-yen Sūtra* as belonging to the second category, arguing that only Ch'an, which is beyond all words and letters, belongs to the first category. The point here is not to determine how the scriptures should be classified, but rather to point out that the two kinds of faith, patriarchal faith and doctrinal faith, as well as the two truths, *paramārtha satya*, or "absolute truth," and *saṃvṛti satya*, or "relative truth," are directly related to the two types of hermeneutic attitude toward the scriptures. Whereas nonbacksliding patriarchal faith and *paramārtha satya* are related to the first category, doctrinal faith and *saṃvṛti satya* are related to the second. Hence, in the final analysis, doctrinal faith is simply *upāya*, or "skill-in-means," used by enlightened teachers for pedagogical purposes at the level of *saṃvṛti satya* in order to adjust the Buddha's teachings to the various capacities of their listeners. Ultimately, however, doctrinal faith must be transformed into nonbacksliding patriarchal faith at the level of *paramārtha satya*.

Part Two
Practice

BODHIDHARMA
Painted in brush and ink by the venerable Korean monk
Song-dahm (1976).

Chapter Seven
The Unity of Faith and Enlightenment in Practice

The mark of true Mahāyāna Buddhist faith is its inseparability from practice and enlightenment. Thus, faith has a threefold structure. However, we can consider this structure from the perspective of both doctrinal and patriarchal faith. In the first case, faith leads to practice and practice leads to enlightenment; in the second, faith *is* practice and practice *is* enlightenment. Since the key point is the inseparability of faith, practice, and enlightenment, both positions seem valid; yet I would argue that patriarchal faith is more in line with basic Buddhist insights concerning the nondual nature of reality.

Doctrinal faith is faith in the possibility of becoming a Buddha through a long process of gradual practice. In contrast, as soon as patriarchal faith is aroused, enlightenment is instantly attained. Consequently, when one has patriarchal faith, practice is not a preliminary to enlightenment, but is instead a *function* of enlightenment. In other words, the doctrinal method of practice presupposes a dualistic subject–object (*neng-so*) construction, whereas the patriarchal method of practice presupposes a nondual essence–function (*t'i-yung*) construction. Doctrinal faith establishes a dualism between sentient beings and Buddha, and then an attempt must be made to bridge this gap through gradual practice. In contrast, the tradition of sudden enlightenment argues that, no matter how determined they are, practitioners having only doctrinal faith cannot remove the distinction between themselves and Buddha, because this gap does not in fact exist. It is simply a false distinction made by the discriminating mind. Consequently, the only way to eliminate this presumed gap is to realize that it does not actually exist. Gradual practice is regarded by the school of sudden enlightenment as a mere extension of the dualistic way of thinking, which functions only to postpone our enlightenment until the future. Thus, the suddenists argue that enlightenment can never be attained by gradual practices based on a doctrinal faith.

When one understands practice not as a preliminary to enlightenment as in the *neng-so* construction of doctrinal faith, but as a natural expression of enlightenment as in the *t'i-yung* construction of patriarchal faith, then there exists a perfect unity between practice and enlightenment. The doctrine concerning the unity of practice and enlightenment (Japanese: *shushō-ichinyo*) was given perhaps its most famous expression by the Japanese Sōtō Zen master Dōgen in his *Shōbōgenzō*:

The view that practice and enlightenment are not one is heretical. In the Buddhadharma they are one. Inasmuch as practice is based on enlightenment, the practice of even a novice is all of original enlightenment. Thus, in giving instructions for practice, a Zen master advises his disciples not to seek enlightenment beyond practice, for practice itself is original enlightenment.[1]

The key statement here is "not to seek enlightenment beyond practice for practice itself is original enlightenment." According to Dōgen, the practice of Zen or Ch'an is "practice based on enlightenment" (*shōjō no shu*) and not "practice prior to enlightenment" (*shōzen no shu*). He therefore says:

Śākyamuni Buddha and Mahākāśyapa lived by practice based on enlightenment (*shōjō no shu*); Bodhidharma and Hui-neng were also guided by practice based on enlightenment. There is no exception in the way Dharma has been kept alive.[2]

The inseparability of practice and enlightenment attributed by Dōgen to the first patriarch Bodhidarma is analyzed at length in the following chapter in terms of *pi-kuan*, or "wall meditation." However, this unity is also discussed by the sixth patriarch Hui-neng in his *Platform Sūtra* in terms of the inseparable nature of meditation (*ting*) and wisdom (*hui*). In explaining his theory of sudden enlightenment by sudden practice (*tun-wu tun-hsiu*), Hui-neng writes:

Good friends, my teaching of the Dharma takes meditation [*ting*] and wisdom [*hui*] as its basis. Never under any circumstances say mistakenly that meditation and wisdom are different; they are a unity, not two things. Meditation is the essence [*t'i*] of wisdom, wisdom itself is the function [*yung*] of meditation. At the very moment when there is wisdom, then meditation exists in wisdom; at the very moment when there is meditation, then wisdom exists in meditation. Good friends, this means that meditation and wisdom are alike. Students, be careful not to say that meditation gives rise to wisdom, or that wisdom gives rise to meditation, or that meditation and wisdom are different from one another. To hold this view implies that things have duality.[3]

Hui-neng describes the indivisible *t'i-yung*, or "essence-function," structure of meditation and wisdom by the analogy of a lamp (*t'i*) and its light (*yung*):

Good friends, how then are meditation and wisdom

[57]

alike? They are like the lamp and the light that it gives forth. If there is a lamp there is light, if there is no lamp there is no light. The lamp is the essence [*t'i*] of light, the light is the function [*yung*] of the lamp. Thus, although they have two names, in essence they are not two. Meditation and wisdom are also like this.[4]

From one perspective, it can be said that meditation (*ting*) or practice (*hsing*) is *t'i*, "essence," whereas wisdom (*hui*) or enlightenment is its *yung*, "function." From another perspective, one might say that enlightenment is *t'i* and practice is its dynamic *yung*. However, as Hui-neng emphasizes in the *Platform Sūtra*: "If you argue which comes first, meditation or wisdom, you are deluded people. You want to be able to settle the argument and instead will cling to objective things." The key point here is that practice and enlightenment are simultaneous. In other words, the *t'i-yung* structure characterizing the relation of practice to enlightenment eliminates the idea of time-sequence but stresses their total inseparability and nonduality. However, it must be cautioned here that many Buddhists practice, and still are not enlightened. Why is it so? The answer here is that practice and enlightenment are indeed inseparable, *but only when based on patriarchal faith*. Hence, patriarchal faith is the secret to successful practice in Buddhism.

Chapter Eight
Bodhidharma's Wall Meditation

Perhaps the most direct way of illustrating what we mean by a practice that is based on true patriarchal faith is to analyze *pi-kuan*, or "wall meditation," which was introduced by Bodhidharma, the first patriarch of Ch'an Buddhism. Bodhidharma sat at the Shao-lin Temple doing *pi-kuan* without interacting with others for nine years.[1] What, precisely, does *pi-kuan* mean? It is crucial to understand this thoroughly since the entire history of Ch'an Buddhism may be described as an elaboration of Bodhidharma's *pi-kuan*. Indeed, Seizan Yanagida, the renowned contemporary Japanese Zen scholar, has written in his book *Zen Thought* that "the history of Ch'an Buddhism is the history of the misunderstanding and wrong evaluation of the term *pi-kuan* or 'wall meditation.' "[2]

One of the common misunderstandings about Bodhidharma's meditation arises from the superficial association of the term *pi-kuan*, which is translated as "wall meditation," with the external sitting posture of Ch'an monks. In Chinese, *pi* means "wall" and *kuan* means "observation"; moreover, it is a fact that, when Ch'an monks meditate, they often sit facing the wall of the meditation hall. However, there is no logical connection between the term *pi-kuan*, or "wall meditation," and gazing at a wall when sitting. The essence of meditation as a practice of patriarchal faith lies in its being a function of Buddha-nature. Buddha-nature, as the *Platform Sūtra* states, is always pure and bright, illuminating everywhere, beyond the *neng-so* construction and beyond the limits of space and time. Therefore, meditation need not be merely "wall" meditation. When one meditates lying down and gazing up at the ceiling, one's meditation should be called "ceiling meditation"; when one is gazing at the floor, it should be called "floor meditation"; when one is walking, it should be "walking meditation"; and so on. Regardless of where one is or what one does, this should be meditation. Why, then, has meditation been called simply "wall meditation" by the patriarchs? At this point we must investigate the symbolic meaning of wall meditation in the Ch'an tradition.

In the *Treatise on the Fourfold Practice through the Twofold Entrance*, the oldest extant work attributed to Bodhidharma, we read:

There are many ways to enter the Path, but briefly speaking they are of two sorts only. The first is *li-ju* or "Entering by communion with primordial reality," and the other is *hsing-ju* or "Entering by practice." Entering by communion with primordial reality is awakening to the essence of Buddhism through the aid of scriptural teaching, giving one deep faith in one's True Nature which is the same in all sentient beings. Only due to false thoughts is it not manifested. Therefore, when a man abandons the false and returns to the true, and firmly abides in *pi-kuan* or wall meditation, he discovers that there is neither self nor other, that the profane and the sacred are one, so that he firmly abides in this state and never moves away therefrom. He will then not be a slave to words, for he is in silent communion with the primordial reality itself, free from conceptual discrimination; he is serene and not-acting. This is called "Entering by communion with primordial reality." "Entering by practice" means the four acts in which all other acts are included. What are the four? (1) To know how to subdue your hatred; (2) To follow

[60]

karma; (3) Not to crave anything; and (4) To be in accord with Dharma."[3]

If the relationship between *li-ju* and *hsing-ju* is taken as the relationship between faith and its practice as indicated in the above passage, then *pi-kuan* functions as a simple action in which both *li-ju* and *hsing-ju*, or faith and its practice, are united. In other words, if there is no faith that all sentient beings have the same true nature, then *pi-kuan* is not possible, just as if there is no *pi-kuan*, then the four practices listed by Bodhidharma are not possible.

Thus, Bodhidharma's *Treatise on Fourfold Practice through the Twofold Entrance* can be interpreted as a text explaining the relationship between patriarchal faith and practice. In terms of the *t'i-yung* construction, *li-ju* as patriarchal faith is *t'i*, or "essence," whereas *hsing-ju* as practice represents its *yung*, or "function." Finally faith and practice are inseparably united in a single act of *pi-kuan*.

Thus, an act of *pi-kuan* involves the following elements:

1. Through the aid of scriptual teachings one can have deep faith that every sentient being has the same true nature, which is described as the content of enlightenment.[4]

2. The *Treatise on Fourfold Practice* warns that, in those who do not have patriarchal faith, this true nature is not manifested because of false thoughts that arise from appearances. Therefore, the controversial phrase *she-wang kuei-chen*, "abandon false thought and return to true nature," must be understood as a prerequisite for wall meditation. It should not be taken to be a form of doctrinal faith that "I can become a Buddha" by abandoning false thoughts and re-

turning to true nature. Rather, it is a rejection of doctrinal faith. That is, "abandoning false thoughts" means nothing but abandoning doctrinal faith. Indeed, as long as one holds onto any residue of doctrinal faith, wall meditation cannot begin.

3. The characterization of wall meditation in the *Treatise on Fourfold Practice* is concluded by the phrase *pu-sui wen-chiao*, "not following after any scriptural teachings."[5]

Traditionally, practice refers to the four kinds of mindfulness, i.e., contemplation of (1) the body (*kāya*) as impure; (2) feeling (*vedanā*) as suffering; (3) mind (*citta*) as empty; and (4) existence (*dharma*) as insubstantial. In order to perceive the impurity of the human body, practitioners used the famous skeleton meditation. From the moment of death until the body is reduced to a skeleton, they observe the process of decomposition. They believe that in this way all of their attachments will be eliminated. What is the ultimate purpose of these practices? It is to become an *arhat*, a Hīnayāna sage.

The most popular form of Buddhist practice consists of the so-called three disciplines: morality (*śīla*), concentration (*dhyāna*), and wisdom (*prajña*). Another common practice is that of the "six perfections," these being generosity, holding precepts, patience, diligence, meditation, and wisdom. The last two perfections (*pāramitās*), meditation and wisdom, are also frequently referred to as the practices of *śamatha* and *vipaśyanā*, "quiescence" and "insight."

The practice of patriarchal faith in an act of *pi-kuan* does not negate the value of all these other traditional practices; to good Buddhists they are elementary. Still, it is wrong to think that one can become Buddha through such practices. Rather, all the merits that one accumulates by practicing the four kinds of mindfulness, the three disciplines, and the six perfections along with *sámatha-vipaśyanā* can be acquired in a single act of *pi-kuan* on the basis of patriarchal faith.

Let us examine the term *pi-kuan* as it is developed in Bodhidharma's treatise. The phrase preceding the term *pi-kuan* is *ning-chu*, literally meaning "abiding firmly." Therefore, the term *pi-kuan* acquires a fuller sense in the context of the complete phrase *ning-chu pi-kuan*, "abiding firmly in wall meditation." Here, the Chinese character *pi*, or "wall," is used as an *upamā*, or analogy, wherein *ning-chu* is its *upameya*, i.e., that to which it is being compared. In other words, *pi-kuan* can be called *ning-chu kuan*, "abiding firmly in meditation," without its *upamā*, i.e., *pi*, or "wall." If this analysis based on the traditional Buddhist *upamā–upameya* construction is acceptable, the meaning of *ning-chu*, or "abiding firmly," becomes crucial for our correct understanding of the controversial term *pi-kuan*. The contemporary Japanese Zen scholar, Seizan Yanagida, provides a very insightful interpretation of the term *ning-chu*:

> The Chinese term *ning-chu* [Japanese: *gyōnen to shite*] refers to the way of being of a person who has abandoned the false and returned to the true, who abides firmly without moving in the state in which both self and other or the profane and sacred are one and who is no longer a slave to words *Ning-chu* is the term describing the surprise of a person who beholds the primordial being which he has found. In the term *ning-chu*, we see the moving tone of a person who is now facing the real truth which is beyond life and death or survival and perishing.[6]

In Buddhist literature, *ning* usually refers to the state of nondiscrimination or nonduality. Therefore, the word *ning-chu* can be understood to mean "abiding firmly in nondiscrimination." By the placement of the Chinese character *pi* after the word *ning-chu*, Bodhidharma's meditation practice becomes more picturesque. In Asian culture, the wall is a symbol of no compromise, no negotiation, and no change whatever as well as of great strength, trust, and wisdom. Moreover, since a wall sees both sides, as it were, it is a symbol of nonduality and nondiscrimination. There is thus no better term than *pi* as a simile for *ning-chu*.

Finally, the word *ning-chu* is directly related to the concept of Buddhist "faith" as *śraddhā*, which is the act of sustaining confidence, remaining steadfast, or sustaining one's trust in the sense of abiding firmly. Consequently, *ning-chu* may be understood to represent faith as "abiding firmly" or "remaining steadfast" in a state of nondiscrimination and nonduality. Hence, in the final analysis, the phrase *ning-chu kuan* can be considered a combination of *ning-chu*, in its sense as "faith" or "abiding firmly," and *kuan*, or "meditation," so as to signify the total inseparability of faith and practice. The complete phrase *ning-chu pi-kuan* then comes to mean "abiding firmly in faith through nondual meditation like a wall."

Yanagida gives a very insightful interpretation of *pi-kuan* which emphasizes *prajñā*, or "wisdom," in such a way that the usual understanding of *pi-kuan* is reversed. His translation of *pi-kuan* into Japanese as *kabe ga miru* does not mean "wall gazing" or "wall observation," as is usually understood by the term, but instead means "wall sees" or "wall observes." Therefore, whereas the traditional interpretation of *pi-kuan* emphasizes *pi* as the object of one's seeing, Yanagida's interpretation places emphasis on *kuan* or the act of seeing *like* a wall, which means "abiding firmly in a nondual state of wisdom." Yanagida then asks, "What does a wall see?" It sees the emptiness of all things, the emptiness of self as well as others.

Thus, according to Yanagida, *pi-kuan* is a wide-open meditation. Any meditation in which one's mind can be like a wall as defined by Bodhidharma can be called wall meditation, regardless of one's posture or the place where one is practicing. Therefore, Bodhidharma's contribution to the sixth century Buddhist world in China was to provide a standard that could be applied to all Buddhist meditation practices. In other words, *pi-kuan* is not a specific kind of meditation but establishes the *criteria* of meditation and right practice, namely (1) a deep faith that all sentient beings have the same true nature, (2) a state of mind that is like a wall, i.e., "abiding firmly" in a state of nondualism, and (3) a constant mindfulness of the fourfold practices in one's daily life.

Chapter Nine
Questioning Meditation and the Dynamics of Faith

Although faith is often conceived of as a static state, i.e., as pure affirmation, Buddhist faith, in its deepest sense as nonbacksliding patriarchal faith, is a living activity that is thoroughly dynamic in structure. This dynamic structure involves a kind of dialectic tension between affirmation and negation or faith and doubt, so that the idea of doubt is always intrinsic in an act of faith. This is especially manifest in what the Ch'an tradition terms "questioning meditation" (Chinese: *kung-an*; Korean: *kong'an*; Japanese: *kōan*), which has been popularized in the West under its Japanese name as *kōan* practice.[1]

If it is true that "I am Buddha," then why is practice necessary? In fact, the state of mind of most practitioners involves a major conflict between the backsliding doctrinal faith of *aniyata rāśi*, the "undetermined class," and the nonbacksliding patriarchal faith of *niyata rāśi*, the "determined class." Whereas the nonbacksliding patriarchal faith of *niyata rāśi* affirms that "I am already Buddha," the backsliding doctrinal faith of *aniyata rāśi* holds that "I can become Buddha," which of course involves the confession that "I am not Buddha" or "I am an ignorant sentient being." Therefore, doctrinal faith represents the state of doubt or negation that stands in dialectic opposition to patriarchal faith, or the state of affirmation. Since most practitioners cannot reject the patriarchal faith that "I am Buddha," yet must also confess that "I am not Buddha," an inner conflict between these two poles of faith and doubt or affirmation and negation is created. How can this be resolved?

When patriarchal faith is understood to be not a mere static affirmation but a dynamic model of faith, then both extremes of affirmation and negation or faith and doubt are seen to be involved in each act of patriarchal faith. Thus, doctrinal faith is actually intrinsic in patriarchal faith. Consequently, the Ch'an tradition invented the practice of questioning meditation, which resolves this inner contradiction not by emphasizing one pole or the other, but by activating and intensifying the polarity through a process of unbroken questioning. For this reason, an analysis of the Ch'an process of questioning meditation can help us to understand the dynamics of patriarchal faith in Buddhism.[2]

The dynamics of patriarchal faith operating in the process of questioning meditation can best be approached theoretically by means of the "three essentials" of kung-an, or "questioning practice," introduced by the fourteenth century Ch'an master Kao-feng (1326–1396) in his influential book Ch'an-yao, or The Essentials of Ch'an Meditation.

> For serious meditation one needs three essentials: the first essential is to have a great faith as if one is sitting on Mt. Sumeru; the second essential is to have a strong determination as if one has met the enemy who had killed one's father and would immediately wish to attack; the third essential is to have an immense questioning as if one were carrying out the most important activity in his life in a dark place.[3]

In his popular book entitled The Three Pillars of

Zen, Philip Kapleau makes a slight adjustment of Kao-feng's three essentials of *kung-an* or *koan* meditation:

> The first of the three essentials of Zen practice is a strong faith (*dai-shinkon*). This is more than mere belief. The ideogram for *kon* means "root," and that for *shin*, "faith." Hence, the phrase implies a faith that is firmly and deeply rooted, immovable, like an immense tree or a huge boulder . . . . The second indispensable quality is a feeling of strong doubt (*dai-gidan*) . . . . It is a doubt as to why we and the world appear so imperfect, so full of anxiety, strife and suffering, when in fact our deep faith tells us exactly the opposite is true. It is a doubt which leaves us no rest . . . . strong doubt, therefore, exists in proportion to strong faith . . . . In Zen, "doubt" implies not skepticism but a state of perplexity, of probing inquiry, of intense self-questioning. From this feeling of doubt the third essential, strong determination (*dai-funshi*), naturally arises. It is an overwhelming determination to dispel doubt with the whole force of our energy or will.[4]

Although different formulations of the three essentials of Ch'an practice are obviously possible, the meaning is clear: Ch'an involves an intense struggle between faith and doubt, affirmation and negation, "I am Buddha" and "I am not Buddha," which is resolved in a single, determined act of inward questioning. As Kapleau clarifies, the meaning of "doubt" in its Zen or Ch'an context is not one of skepticism but of questioning. However, one must not be led by Kapleau's formulation of the three essentials to think that questioning is simply the second dialectic moment opposing deep faith; for as Kao-feng's formulation makes clear, the immense questioning is actually the third moment of the three essentials and results from the tension between great faith and great doubt. This structure of the three essentials activating the dynamics of Ch'an patriarchal faith in questioning meditation is illustrated by the following diagram:

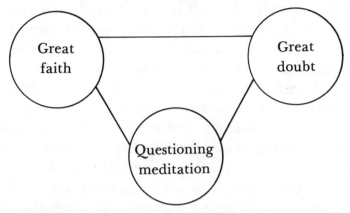

The dynamic concept of Buddhist patriarchal faith resembles in certain respects the dynamic models of faith developed by the famous Existential Protestentant theologians Sören Kierkegaard (1813-1855) and Paul Tillich (1866-1965). The Mahāyāna Buddhist contrast between doctrinal and patriarchal faith is seen in Kierkegaard's well-known distinction between faith as passionate inwardness or subjectivity, and objective or doctrinal faith. Kierkegaard argues that objective knowledge is the dialectical negation of faith and opposes the subjectivity of faith. Faith tends to become reasoned and objective so that it must be constantly interiorized. The existing individual is incommensurate with objective reality so that to know objectively is to cease to exist subjectively. Existence in faith is antithetical to existence in objective reality. Therefore, in contrast to what Kierkegaard terms "objective faith," understood as a "sum of doctrinal propositions," true faith is a "passionate inwardness," whose subjectivity negates objectivity.[5] In his theology of faith, Kierkegaard maintains that the basis of all misinterpretations of Christianity is the objectification of faith, i.e., the transformation of authentic faith as passionate inwardness into mere doctrinal faith. Thus, in his work entitled, *Concluding Unscientific Postscript*, he states: "Faith constitutes a sphere all by itself, and every misunderstanding of Christianity may at once be recognized by its transforming it into a doctrine, transferring it to the sphere of the intellectual."[6]

In describing man's assent to true faith as passionate inwardness, Kierkegaard outlines three stages of life — aesthetic, moral and religious — whereby escaping from the material world, one unites himself by choice with the Infinite, through a radical "leap of faith." That is to say, using faith as a springboard, so to speak, one makes a daring leap whereby one immediately passes into Infinity. This "leap of faith" of which Kierkegaard speaks, indicates the *sudden* nature of salvation through faith as passionate inwardness, in contrast to the gradual process of doctrinal investigation undertaken by objective knowledge. In Kierkegaard's own words:

> The existing individual who chooses to pursue the objective way enters upon the entire approximation process by which it proposed to bring God to light objectively. But this is in all eternity impossible, because God is a subject, and therefore exists only for subjectivity in inwardness. The existing individual who chooses the subjective way apprehends instantly the dialectical difficulty involved in having to use some time, perhaps a long time, in finding God objectively; and he feels this dialectical difficulty in all its painfulness, because every moment is wasted in which he does not have God. That very instant he has God, not by virtue of any objective deliberation, but by virtue of the infinite passion of inwardness. The objective inquirer, on the other hand, is not embarrassed by such dialectical difficulties as are involved in devoting an

entire period of investigation to finding God . . . . Here is where the way swings off, and the change is marked by the fact that while objective knowledge rambles comfortably on by way of the long road of approximation without being impelled by the urge of passion, subjective knowledge counts every delay a deadly peril . . . .[7]

According to Kierkegaard, true faith is an infinite, passionate and personal commitment to Christ, the "God-Man." Yet, the notion of Christ as a "God-Man," i.e., as a union of eternity and time, is a "paradox" or "absurdity" to the intellect, and therefore creates an "objective uncertainity." However, it is exactly here that we find the "dynamic" aspect of faith in Kierkegaard's theology. For Kierkegaard states that objective uncertainty and subjective passion create a tension or dynamic interplay, so that the greater our objective uncertainty, the more intense becomes our subjective passion and inwardness. Thus, Kierkegaard defines faith as . . . . "An objective uncertainty held fast in an appropriation-process of the most passionate inwardness."[8] Again, he states: "Without risk there is no faith. Faith is precisely the contradiction between the infinite passion of the individual's inwardness and the objective uncertainty."[9]

This dynamic model of faith articulated in Kierkegaard's existential thought was later developed by the eminent twentieth century protestant theologian Paul Tillich. In his classic book entitled *Dynamics of Faith*, Tillich defines faith as "the state of being ultimately concerned." So defined, "doubt" now becomes intrinsic to each act of faith. Tillich writes: "If faith is understood as belief that something is true, it is incompatible with the act of faith. If faith is understood as being ultimately concerned, doubt is a necessary element in it." Tillich argues, however, that the "doubt" implicit in every act of faith is not the methodological doubt of a scientist or the doubt of a skeptic, but an "existential doubt":

The doubt which is implicit in every act of faith is neither the methodological nor the skeptical doubt . . . . One could call it the existential doubt, in contrast to the methodological or skeptical doubt. It does not question whether a special proposition is true or false. It does not reject every concrete truth, but is aware of the element of insecurity in every existential truth.[10]

Thus understood, faith and doubt are poles of a single act of ultimate concern. "If doubt appears, it should not be considered as the negation of faith, but as an element which was always and will always be present in the act of faith. Existential doubt and faith are poles of the same reality, the state of ultimate concern."[11]

It is this dialectical tension between faith and doubt in each act of ultimate concern that Tillich defines as the dynamic model of faith:

The "dynamics of faith" are present not only in the inner tensions and conflicts of the content of faith, but also present in the life of man. Where there is faith there is tension between participation and separation, between the faithful one and his ultimate concern. . . . All this is said of living faith, of faith as actual concern, and not of faith as a traditional attitude without tensions, without doubt and without courage.[12]

Tillich's faith involves a "courage to be," or a courageous determination to affirm one's true being in God, which involves a dialectical overcoming of "nonbeing," i.e., the existential moment of doubt, estrangement or alienation, guilt, and meaninglessness. Thus, Tillich says, "Courage as an element of faith is the daring self-affirmation of one's being in spite of the powers of 'nonbeing'."[13]

In Buddhism, a dynamic model of faith including the "courage to be" would involve the determined self-affirmation of one's original Buddhahood in the face of an existential doubt or objective uncertainty such as "I am an ignorant sentient being." Buddhist Mahāyāna Faith is dynamic because it is not a static affirmation, a simple yes-saying, but a tension between the two poles of affirmation and negation, of faith and doubt, or what the famous Ch'an master Wu-men (1183–1260) called "a moment of yes-and-no."[14] Therefore, in the dynamics of patriarchal faith, there is a faith-doubt dialectic, wherein doubt does not cancel faith, but instead acts as a "fuel," causing the flame of faith to burn brighter and higher.

In contrast to Kierkegaard's and Tillich's models of dynamic faith, however, the Mahāyāna Buddhist model becomes manifest in a specific *practice*, namely *kung-an* or *koan* meditation. Through the active questioning process of *kung-an* meditation, the faith-doubt dialectic is activated and brought to its extreme limit, culminating in the enlightenment experience of "brokenness," as described in the final chapters of this work. Furthermore, Kierkegaard and Tillich elaborate their dynamic models of faith in the context of a Christian theistic world-view, whereas patriarchal faith must be understood in the context of the strictly nontheistic world-view of Mahāyāna Buddhism. Thus, there are obvious limitations to the analogy between the Existential Protestant theology of faith and the patriarchal faith of Mahāyāna Buddhism, and it is pointless to press the analogy beyond these limitations.

Nonetheless, the model of faith constructed by such Western thinkers as Kierkegaard and Tillich does indeed allow us to illustrate the crucial dynamics of East Asian *kung-an* or questioning meditation in a manner which I do not believe has ever been made explicit in a theoretic way.

As indicated in the Introduction to this writing, the Kyoto School of Japan has brilliantly described the role of Great Doubt in the realization of Great Enlightenment. According to Keiji Nishitani, in his book *What is Religion?*, when we press our doubt to its extreme limits we extinguish our false "I" or ego into the ground of *nihilum* or absolute nothingness, what Zen Buddhism calls the experience of "Great Death."[15] Here, the distinction between the doubter and the doubted collapses into what Keiji Nishitani calls a "great doubting-mass" wherein reality becomes one big question mark, so to speak. Therefore, this Great Doubt is a deep existential awareness of an unfathomable *nihilum*. However, Nishitani does not adequately demonstrate the dynamic aspect of *koan* meditation in Zen Buddhism as practiced by the Rinzai sects, which as I have argued, involves a dialectical struggle between doubt and faith. Insofar as Nishitani and the Kyoto School do discuss faith, it is always in the sense of Pure Land faith as understood in Shinran's School as other-power faith which comes as a gift of Amida's compassion, or Calvin's Protestant theology where faith is always a gift of God's grace. However, this does not address the dynamics of Zen *koan* meditation. Thus, in order to correct this shortcoming in our understanding of questioning practice, I have tried to develop a framework which shows Great Enlightenment as a result of the tension arising between Great Faith, in its self-power sense as "I am Buddha," and

Great Doubt, as the negation of this as expressed by the phrase "I am an ignorant sentient being."

There are about 1,700 *kung-ans* in the tradition of Ch'an Buddhism. Each of these contains some hidden message of the Ch'an masters. When a student is given a *kung-an*, he is required to discern the hidden message. Easily the most famous and popular *kung-an* is *wu*, which was given by Ch'an master Chao-chou (778–897). A monk who respected Chao-chou highly asked him a question: "Has a dog the Buddha-nature or not?" Chao-chou said, "*Wu*", meaning "No"! Completely puzzled, the monk thought to himself, "From the highest Buddhas down to the lowliest creatures such as ants, all have the Buddha-nature. Why is it that a dog has not? Why did Chao-chou say "No" [*Wu*]? Why? Why?"[16]

This dialogue appears in many Ch'an books, and there have been many attempts to interpret it. One of the most influential commentaries is that of Wu-men, who writes in the first chapter of his book *Wu-men Kuan*, or *The Gateless Gate*:

In studying Ch'an, one must pass the barrier set up by ancient Ch'an masters. For the attainment of incomparable enlightenment, one has to cast away his discriminating mind. Those who have not passed the barrier and have not cast away the discriminating mind are all phantoms haunting trees and plants. Now, tell me, what is the barrier of the Ch'an master? Just this "*wu*"—it is the only barrier of Ch'an. It is thus called the "gateless barrier of Ch'an." Those who have passed the barrier will not only see Chao-chou clearly, but will go hand in hand with all the masters of the past, see them face to face. You will see with the same eye and hear with the same ear that they do. Wouldn't it be wonderful? Don't you want to pass the barrier? Then concentrate yourself on this *"wu"* with your 360 bones and 84,000 pores, making your whole body one great inquiry.

This passage is followed by a poem:

The dog! The Buddha-nature!
The truth is manifested in full.
A moment of yes-and-no:
Lost are your body and soul.[17]

Every sentence in Wu-men's commentary has become a classical statement in the study of Ch'an. However, we should realize that any interpretation of the *kung-an*, no matter how precise or beautiful it may be, is useless for the questioning meditation itself and can even be an obstruction. For the *kung-an* meditation it is crucial to maintain a constant, unbroken questioning of *wu*. The key to the *kung-an* is not the word *wu*, but the active process of questioning itself, i.e., "Why? Why? Why?" It is for this reason that the faith–doubt dialectic is activated in the dynamic questioning process of *kung-an* Ch'an meditation. Ultimately, the purpose of the questioning meditation is to "cast away [one's] discriminating mind," as Wu-men declares, so that such distinctions as the affirmation that "I am Buddha" and the negation that "I am not Buddha" are eliminated. Another questioning meditation attributed to Chao-chou illustrates this very well. A different monk asked Chao-chou, "Has a dog the Buddha-nature or not?" This time the master said, "Yes!" In the biography of Wei-k'uan (755-817), we read:

A monk asked, "Has a dog the Buddha-nature or not?" The master said, "Yes." The monk again asked, Have

you the Buddha-nature or not? The master said, "No!"
The monk therefore inquired: "All sentient beings have
the Buddha-nature. Why is it that you alone have
not?"[18]

The true barrier in Ch'an is thus the discriminating
mind itself; whether one says yes or no is irrelevant.
Through Ch'an questioning meditation, the
faith–doubt or affirmation–negation dialectic, i.e., the
inner tension between "I am Buddha" and "I am not
Buddha," completely breaks down when the
discriminating mind is cast away until at last:

The truth is manifested in full.
A moment of yes-and-no.[19]

Chapter Ten
Practice in the Treatise
on Awakening Mahāyāna Faith

The most classical treatment of faith in Mahāyāna Buddhism is the *Ta-ch'eng ch'i-hsin lun*, or *Treatise on Awakening Mahāyāna Faith*. As the title indicates, the basic theme of the treatise is awakening Mahāyāna faith. One might initially wonder whether faith is actually of central concern since the nature of faith is not explicitly discussed until the end of the work. However, a deeper examination of the text reveals three basic kinds of faith: The first type is alluded to throughout the first, second, and third chapters and is the faith of the title of the text. The second type is discussed at the beginning of the fourth chapter, entitled "On Faith and Practice". The third type is briefly described at the end of the fourth chapter, and is the faith in Amitābha Buddha. The treatise is systematically arranged in order to aid people of differing capacities. First *cheng hsin*, or "right faith" is discussed. This is the faith of *niyata rāśi*, the "determined class," who have *pu-t'ui hsin*, or "nonbacksliding faith." Next, for those unable to grasp the first type of faith, i.e., *aniyata rāśi*, the "undetermined class," having only *t'ui hsin*, or "backsliding faith," a second type of faith is described in terms of the famous theory of four faiths and five practices. Finally, for those unable to practice even the second type of faith, *nien-fo*, or recitation of the name of Amitābha Buddha while wishing for rebirth in Pure Land, is recommended. However, the general theme of the treatise is the perfection of one's faith, so that it is transformed from the backsliding faith of the undetermined class to the nonbacksliding faith of the determined class—in other words, so that it is transformed from *hsin-hsin*, which is the "mind of faith," into *fa-hsin*, which is "*bodhi*-mind" or the "mind of wisdom."

The first kind of faith described in the treatise can be called simply One Mind Faith and, again, is the faith of the title. As emphasized by Wŏnhyo, the term *ta-ch'eng*, or "*Mahāyāna*," refers to *i-hsin*, or "One Mind," which is "the Mind of all sentient beings." In other words, we can render the title as *Awakening the Mind of Faith*. We thus conclude that the title of the treatise simply means "the naturally functioning mind" or "the properly working mind."

A simpler way of reading the title is to follow the order of the Chinese characters, *Ta-ch'eng ch'i-hsin*, which means "Mahāyāna arouses faith" or, again, "Mind arouses faith." This is consistent with one of the first sentences of the treatise: "There is One Thing which can arouse the root of Mahāyāna faith." The treatise specifies that the term One Thing refers to One Mind or the Mind of sentient beings. Therefore, this sentence actually means "There is a Mind which can arouse the root of Mahāyāna faith." Here, Mind is *t'i*, or "essence," and faith is its *yung*, or "function"; that is, One Mind and faith cannot be separated. In his *Haedongso*, Wŏnhyo comments on this statement as follows:

The words "there is One Thing," which begin the first [section of this part of the treatise] refer to the truth of One Mind. If people are able to understand this truth, they are bound to arouse the broad and great root of faith. Hence the words, "which can arouse the root of Mahāyāna faith." The marks of the root of faith are like [the description of faith given in] the explanation of the title. When the root of faith is established, [one] immediately enters Buddha's way. Having entered Buddha's way, [one] obtains inexhaustible treasure.[1]

Since the "root of faith" is aroused by returning to One Mind, the key point of the *Treatise on Awakening Mahāyāna Faith* according to Wŏnhyo and many other commentators is the return to One Mind. Moreover, Wŏnhyo directly relates the root of faith to his analysis of the text's title in terms of the essence–function construction, where One Mind is essence and faith its function. Therefore, according to the treatise, faith is not a function of will, reason, or other fallible psychological faculties, but of One Mind, which means that it is grounded in the ontological reality of Suchness itself. If the treatise is correct, then it is indeed possible to claim a nonbacksliding faith, as was argued in an earlier section.

The true mark of Buddhist faith is that it is *manifested in practice*. A faith that is not expressed through practice, including diligence in meditation, compassion (*karuṇā*), and giving (*dāna*) is impotent. Therefore, faith may be said to have a *circular* nature: It leads to practice, which in turn leads to enlightenment. From the more radical viewpoint of sudden enlightenment, faith *is* practice, practice *is* enlightenment and enlightenment is faith. In *Haedongso* Wŏnhyo describes the importance of this inseparability of faith and practice:

Based on the explanation [of the principle of Mahāyāna], faith will arise; [this faith] must [then] be put into practice, because to have understanding

[80]

without practice is not in accord with the intent of [this] treatise.[2]

Wŏnhyo states that, when we return to One Mind, our faith grows; a faith that is static cannot be real faith. To say that "faith grows" is simply to say that "the mind functions properly." Thus, to have continually growing faith is to have a properly functioning mind that is free of all hindrances and obstructions. What are the hindrances that block the mind's natural functioning and keep one's faith from growing? Traditional Buddhist texts refer to them as *kleśas*, or "defilements." Nearly all Buddhist practices focus on eliminating *kleśas*, since it is believed that only when they are removed can the mind return to its original state and function properly and only then can one's faith grow.

How, according to the *Treatise on Awakening Mahāyāna Faith*, can a practitioner make his faith grow? How can his mind be made to function properly? And how can he eliminate his *kleśas*? The answer is *li-nien*: He must become "free of thoughts." It is one's stream of deluded thoughts that constitutes the *kleśas* obstructing the mind and keep one's faith from growing. How is this so? Here, "thoughts" mean *discriminating* tendencies; it is one's habit of discrimination that prevents the mind from functioning correctly. In the text the state of "no-thought," or *li-nien*, is termed *pen-chiao*, or "original enlightenment," whereas the state of discrimination is called *pu-chiao*, or "nonenlightenment." Nonetheless the state of nonenlightenment and original enlightenment are not separated. In order to explain the movement from nonenlightenment to original enlightenment through *shih-chiao*, or "actualization of enlightenment," the treatise makes use of the famous *Abhidharma* theory of the "four marks" observed in all conditioned *dharmas*: *jāti*, "arising"; *sthiti*, "abiding"; *anyathātva*, "changing"; and *nirodha*, "ceasing."[3] Our thoughts or habits of discrimination (*vikalpa*) also come and go in this order, i.e., *jāti, sthiti, anyathātva,* and *nirodha*. Corresponding to these four marks of thought are four stages of enlightenment related to the four stages of no-thought:

1. Being free of all discrimination (*vikalpa*) as soon as the thought arises at its *jāti*, or arising, stage, called "final enlightenment."
2. Being free of discrimination when the thought arrives at its second stage of *sthiti*, or "abiding," called "approximate enlightenment."
3. Being free of discrimination when the thought arrives at its third stage of *anyathātva*, or changing, called "enlightenment in appearance."
4. Being free of discrimination after the thought has completed its fourth stage of *nirodha*, or "cessation," i.e., after the entire thought has come and gone, called "nonenlightenment" (since it is now too late to be free of discrimination).[4]

The aim of meditation on the four marks of thought is to realize what the treatise terms "final enlightenment," which is equivalent to "original enlightenment." At the level of final enlightenment, one stops discriminating at the first state of *jāti* in order to attain direct insight into the original nature of One Mind, i.e., the mind free of all thoughts. At this stage, one is free of all thoughts because the four marks of thought exist simultaneously, no mark having *svabhāva*, or "self-nature." This direct insight into One Mind in the state of no-thought is termed *chien-sheng*

(Japanese: *kenshō*), which means "enlightenment." At this stage, original enlightenment has become one with the actualization of enlightenment. Finally, the treatise defines the state of final enlightenment as follows: "Since one becomes aware of the original state of our mind, his awareness is called the final enlightenment."

Thus, in the *Treatise on Awakening Mahāyāna Faith*, faith in its highest sense is directly related to the realization of One Mind, which means simply the return to one's original state of mind, i.e., the mind of nonthought and nondiscrimination. In other words, the awakening of Mahāyāna faith means the return to One Mind. However, as the treatise states, One Mind has two aspects and three greatnesses. The two aspects are the Suchness aspect (*chen-ju hsiang*) and the arising–ceasing aspect (*sheng-mieh hsiang*), or the Absolute and phenomenal aspects respectively. In the reality of One Mind, the Absolute and phenomenal aspects of existence cannot be separated: The Absolute is in fact the phenomenal world itself in its Suchness. As stated at the beginning of the third chapter:

> One Mind has two aspects. One is the aspect of Mind in terms of the Absolute [Suchness; *chen-ju*], and the other is the aspect of Mind in terms of phenomena [arising and ceasing; *sheng-mieh*]. Each of these two aspects embraces all states of existence. Why? Because these two aspects are mutually inclusive.[5]

What does the theory of One Mind with two aspects mean in terms of patriarchal faith? Here the treatise establishes the metaphysical foundations of patriarchal faith. To say that the two aspects of Suchness and arising–ceasing are inseparable in the reality of One Mind is simply to say that Buddha and sentient beings are also inseparable. Therefore, to return to One Mind

[83]

and realize the Suchness aspect of all phenomenal things is to obtain a true patriarchal faith that "I am Buddha."

The treatise now explains the two aspects of One Mind in terms of the three greatnesses: *t'i-hsiang-yung*, or the essence, attributes, and functions of One Mind, respectively. Whereas the Absolute aspect of One Mind is said to be *t'i*, "essence," the phenomenal aspect represents its *hsiang*, "attributes," and *yung*, "functions." In *Haedongso*, Wŏnhyo describes three aspects of Mahāyāna faith based on the essence-attributes-functions formula:

> This treatise causes people's faith to be awakened, hence the words, "Awakening Faith." Faith is a term which indicates being certain. What is called [faith means] faith that the principle [of One Mind] really exists, faith that practice can get results, and faith that when practice does get [results] there will be boundless merit. Of these, faith that [the principle of One Mind] really exists is faith in the greatness of "essence" [*t'i*]. Because [we] believe that all dharmas are unobtainable, consequently, [we] believe that there really is the dharma world of equality. Faith that [practice] can get results is faith in the greatness of its "attributes" [*hsiang*]. Because [One Mind] completely possesses the merits of the essence [*t'i*] which permeates [all] sentient beings, consequently [we] believe that because of the permeation of the attributes [*hsiang*] we are bound to return to the Source. Faith in the operation of boundless merit is faith in the greatness of the operation [of One Mind], because there is nothing [that One Mind] does not do. If one can awaken these three faiths, one can enter [the world of] Buddha-dharma, produce all merits, be free from all deviant states, and attain the Peerless Way.[6]

In this analysis "faith" means being *certain* of three truths: (1) that One Mind exists; (2) that practice brings results; and (3) that when practice does bring results, there will be boundless merits. In this sense, faith means removing all doubts and wrong attachments. Wŏnhyo describes the two most destructive of these:

> Sentient beings fall into the sea of life and death for so long and do not hasten to the shore of nirvana only because of doubts and wrong attachments. Therefore, the essence of [what is] here [meant by] saving sentient beings is causing [them] to eliminate [their] doubts and forsake [their] wrong attachments . . . . Two things [specifically] are doubted by those seeking Mahāyāna. The first is doubting the principle, which prevents the production [wisdom] mind; the second is doubting the method, which prevents practice.[7]

Wŏnhyo states that, by establishing the principle of One Mind, one eliminates the first doubt and, by establishing the efficacy of practice, one eliminates the second. As usual, Wŏnhyo emphasizes the need to practice. The mark of true faith is that it leads to practice, which in turn results in the return to One Mind and the production of wisdom. Again, the key theme is the inseparability of faith, practice, and enlightenment in Mahāyāna Buddhism.

We have analyzed patriarchal faith in terms of One Mind with its two aspects and three greatnesses at the level of the nonbacksliding faith of *niyata rāśi*, or the "determined class." We must now analyze the two forms of backsliding faith of *aniyata rāśi*, or the "undetermined class." The second level of faith, which is prescribed in the *Treatise on Awakening Mahāyāna Faith* for those who have not yet returned to One Mind, i.e., the Mind of nonthought and nondiscrimination, is discussed in terms of the well-known theory of four faiths and five practices in the fourth chapter entitled "On Faith and Practice":

Briefly speaking, there are four faiths. What are the four? The first is to believe in the Ultimate Source, in other words, to be mindful, with the utmost willingness, of the principle of Suchness. The second is to believe that the Buddha has innumerable excellent virtues, in other words, to think always of being close to Buddha, to make offerings to him, and to respect him. Furthermore, it means to awaken the capacity for goodness, which is wishing to have the omniscience that the Buddha has. The third is to believe that the Dharma is the source of great benefits, in other words, to think always of practicing all the perfections [*pāramitās*]. The fourth is to believe that the Saṃgha is able to correctly practice the Mahāyāna ideal of benefitting both oneself and others, in other words, to rejoice always in being close to the assembly of Bodhisattvas and to pursue genuine practice as it does.[8]

Thus, the "four faiths" refer simply to a faith in Suchness as well as in the "three treasures," namely, the Buddha, The Dharma, and the Saṃgha. Usually, it is said that a deep faith in the three treasures is the foundation of Buddhist religious life. The treatise is unique in that to this threefold faith in the Buddha, Dharma, and Saṃgha it adds a deep faith in the principle of Suchness. How are we to understand these four faiths philosophically? Actually, the structure of faith in Suchness and the three treasures is the same as that of the first kind of faith discussed above, namely, a faith in One Mind and its three greatnesses, i.e., *t'i-hsiang-yung*, or "essence, attributes, and functions." However, whereas the first kind of faith is directed toward those of the *niyata rāśi*, who have a nonbacksliding faith since they have returned to the original mind of nondiscrimination, the second kind of faith described in terms of Suchness and the three treasures is directed toward those who belong to *aniyata rāśi* who have only backsliding faith. It might therefore be said that the second kind of faith is actually the same as the first, except that it is described in a more externalized and symbolic way for those who have not returned to the original mind of nondiscrimination.

After describing the four faiths in Suchness and the three treasures, the treatise continues: "There are five ways of practice which will enable a man to perfect his faith. They are the practices of charity, precepts, patience, zeal, as well as tranquilization [*śamatha*] and clear observation [*vipaśyanā*]." The treatise refers to five practices, or perfections, rather than six because the last two, *śamatha* and *vipaśyanā* (Chinese: *chih-kuan*), are counted as one. Why are they considered to be one practice? It is simply because in essence they form a unity and must be practiced together. Traditionally, these last two *pāramitās* are said to form the core of the six perfections. The treatise states, "Whether walking, standing, sitting, reclining or rising, one should practice both 'tranquilization' and 'clear insight' side by side." Why is the practice of tranquilization and clear observation so fundamental to one's perfection of faith in Buddhism? In *Haedongso*, Wŏnhyo connects the practice of tranquilization and clear observation to the two aspects of One Mind. When we realize the principle of Suchness, we attain *śamatha*, whereas when we *see* the phenomenal aspect of arising and ceasing as it truly is through the realization of wisdom (*prajñā*), we attain *vipaśyanā*:

The revelation of the Two Aspects [of One Mind] removes [all] doubt. It clarifies that although teaching methods are many, there are not more than two methods in first beginning to practice. Based on the aspect of Suchness the practice of "tranquilization" [śamatha] is cultivated, and based on the aspect of arising and ceasing the practice of "clear observation" [vipaśyanā] is begun. If both tranquilization and clear observation are practiced, myriad practices are thereby performed. If [one] embarks on these two methods, [one] is practicing all other methods. [By thinking] like this [one] eliminates doubts and can begin to practice.[9]

Thus, the practice of tranquilization results in realization of the Suchness aspect of One Mind, which is its *t'i*, or "essence," whereas the practice of clear observation results in realization of the true nature of the arising and ceasing aspect of One Mind, which is its *hsiang*, or "attributes," and *yung*, or "functions." Consequently, the practice of tranquilization and clear observation is the means of perfecting one's faith in One Mind and its three greatnesses of essence, attributes, and functions, which, in more symbolic terms, is faith in Suchness and the three treasures of Buddha, Dharma, and Saṃgha.

In summary it can be said that in the *Treatise on Awakening Mahāyāna Faith*, patriarchal faith, the affirmation that "I am Buddha," is described in detail as a deep faith in One Mind in terms of its two aspects (Suchness/arising-ceasing), Three Greatnesses (essence, attributes, and functions), Four Faiths (Suchness and the three treasures), Five Practices (charity, precepts, patience, zeal, as well as tranquilization and clear observation).

Finally, at the end of the fourth chapter of the treatise, a third kind of faith is briefly discussed. This is faith in Amitābha Buddha, which is prescribed for those who are incapable of practicing even the second kind of faith described above. For these people, the practice of *nien-fo*, or reciting Amitābha's name while wishing for rebirth in Pure Land, is recommended as the easiest and simplest means of cultivation. However, the role of faith in Pure Land *nien-fo* practice is so central that a separate section has been reserved for this topic.

Chapter Eleven
Faith and Practice in Pure Land Buddhism

One of the gravest misinterpretations of Buddhist doctrines is the assumption that Ch'an is the supreme teaching for people at the highest level of spiritual development whereas Pure Land is designed for people at a lower level who are incapable of true meditation. This misinterpretation seems to be supported by *Treatise on Awakening Mahāyāna Faith* itself which states at the end of the fourth chapter:

> Next, suppose there is a man who learns this teaching for the first time and wishes to seek the correct faith but lacks courage and strength. Because he lives in this world of suffering, he fears that he will not always be able to meet the Buddhas and honor them personally, and that, faith being difficult to perfect, he will be inclined to fall back. He should know that the Tathāgatas have an excellent expedient means by which they can protect his faith: that is, through the strength of wholehearted meditation on the Buddha, he will in fulfillment of his wishes be able to be born in the Buddhahood beyond, to see the Buddha always, and to be forever separated from the evil states of existence. It is as the sūtra says: "If a man meditates wholly on Amitābha Buddha in the world of the Western Paradise and wishes to be born in that world, directing all the goodness he has cultivated [toward that goal], then he will be born there." Because he will see the Buddha at all times, he will never fall back. If he meditates on the Dharmakāya, the Suchness of the

Buddha, and with diligence keeps practicing [the meditation], he will be able to be born there in the end because he abides in the correct samādhi.[1]

However, in the statement "Suppose there is a man who learns this teaching for the first time and wishes to seek the correct faith but lacks courage and strength," to whom is the treatise referring? Is it not all sentient beings who have not yet obtained "correct faith," i.e., a nonbacksliding patriarchal faith, and realized their identity with Buddha? Actually, Pure Land *nien-fo*, or recitation of Amitābha Buddha's name, is prescribed by the treatise as an easy, yet effective and fundamental practice for attaining a nonbacksliding or unretrogressive faith: "Because he will see the Buddha at all times, he will never fall back." Therefore, we should eliminate any artificial distinction between people of "lower" and "higher" levels of spiritual achievement and understand that the recitation of Amitābha Buddha's name is applicable to all practitioners as "an excellent expedient means" of protecting one's faith and giving one "correct samādhi."

Let us ask again whether Pure Land Buddhism is actually designed for hopeless "lower level" people. In order to answer this question, let us consider a moment the life of Wŏnhyo, without question the most highly regarded scholar and saint of Korea. According to Wŏnhyo's biographer, he was a prodigy who began his spiritual life as a seeker concentrating on Hua-yen Buddhism. Later, he undertook an exhaustive study of all other Buddhist schools and texts, although in the last years of his life he dedicated himself completely to Pure Land practice. It is said that because of Wŏnhyo all Koreans came to recite the name of Amitābha Buddha. What can we learn from this story? The more Wŏnhyo practiced Buddhism the deeper became his understanding of Pure Land Buddhism. The more his understanding of Buddhism developed, the lower he placed his own level of attainment. When Wŏnhyo practiced Pure Land Buddhism, he called himself a total outcast, far beneath the lowest of people. This relization of his low status was considered to be one of the great awakenings in Wŏnhyo's life. Thereafter, he diligently applied himself to Pure Land recitation practice.[2]

Pure Land and Ch'an Buddhism seem to be opposite schools, at least on the surface. Pure Land Buddhism is called the path of "other-power" (Japanese: *tariki*), which advocates total dependence on the grace of Amitābha Buddha, the lord of Pure Land, whereas Ch'an Buddhism is called the path of "self-power" (*jiriki*), which advocates complete reliance on one's Mind. Whereas Pure Land emphasizes a deep faith in Amitābha's forty-eight primal vows, Ch'an emphasizes a patriarchal faith that "I am Buddha." Pure Land stresses that faith is a gift of Amitābha Buddha's grace and compassion, while Ch'an cultivates a faith of "firmly abiding," which involves one's own efforts. Thus, in contrast to Ch'an, which emphasizes the volitional aspects of faith, such as resoluteness, conviction, and steadfastness, as well as the cognitive aspects, such as belief that one's own Mind is Buddha, Pure Land stresses the purely emotional aspects of faith, such as wholehearted love for and devotion to Amitābha Buddha, which bring great bliss and happiness through Amitābha's blessings. In terms of practice, Ch'an values silent meditation, whereas Pure Land prescribes recitation of the name of Amitābha Buddha. Ch'an emphasizes the importance of awakening here and now, whereas Pure Land emphasizes the importance of being born into Pure Land.

The strongest expression of Pure Land as a path of pure "other-power" was developed by the great

Japanese saint Shinran (1173–1262), especially in his *Kyōgyōshinshō*, or *Treatise on Teaching, Practice, Faith, and Enlightenment*.[3] Shinran emphasized that we must realize our state of total impotence and our need to rely completely on Amitābha (Japanese: Amida) Buddha's primal vows to save all sentient beings. He therefore rejected any form of self-power as a means of salvation; faith was its primary cause. The key idea in his doctrine of faith is that one cannot acquire faith through one's own conviction or efforts; it is a gift of Amitābha Buddha's grace and compassion that arises in the heart of one who is reciting Amitābha's name. According to Shinran, then, only because Amitābha Buddha has given one faith as a gift of grace can it alone be the sole cause of salvation. Consequently, Shinran's revolutionary doctrine of Pure Land faith is comparable to the doctrine of the Protestant reformers Luther and Calvin, which holds that salvation is possible only to those who admit to living in a state of sinfulness and have complete faith in Christ's power of redemption, this faith being purely a gift of God's almighty grace.

Thus far, it appears that Pure Land Buddhism, especially the extreme other-power path advocated by Shinran in Japan, is the opposite of the self-power path of Ch'an Buddhism, which emphasizes sole reliance on one's Mind. However, from the standpoint of salvation, the truly interesting question is not one of self-power (*jiriki*) versus other-power (*tariki*), but one of patriarchal faith versus doctrinal faith. The point here is that, in Buddhism, right practice and right enlightenment require right faith, i.e., patriarchal faith. However, patriarchal faith can be developed from the viewpoint of either self-power or other-power. The criterion of patriarchal faith is not self-power or other-power, but *pu-t'ui*, "nonretrogression" or "nonbacksliding." Since the most important consequence of patriarchal faith is sudden enlightenment, it is the sudden and unretrogressive quality of our faith, not its self-power or other-power orientation, that determines whether it is patriarchal or doctrinal.

In Pure Land practice, as in Ch'an practice, the basic concern is to acquire a nonbacksliding faith and to become a member of *niyata rāśi*, the "determined class." As stated in the *Treatise on Awakening Mahāyāna Faith*, to be reborn in Amitābha Buddha's country is to abide in the company of the determined class in a state of nonretrogression. The reason for this is Amitābha Buddha's eleventh vow. The Buddha is recorded as describing this vow in the *Amidakyō*, or *Amitābha Sūtra*, as follows:

> Buddha declared to Ānanda: "Of the beings who are born into that country [Pure Land], all of them abide in the company of the determined class. Why? Because in that Buddhaland there are none belonging to evil or unassured groups."

Elsewhere, the *Amitābha Sūtra* states:

> Further Śariputra, in the Land of Bliss, beings born there are all in the state of non-retrogression.[4]

Clearly, according to the *Amitābha Sūtra*, to be born in Amitābha Buddha's Pure Land is to acquire a nonbacksliding faith and to join the class of determined ones. When is one born into the Pure Land? This has always been a source of great dispute. Some texts seem to suggest that one takes birth in the Pure Land only after death. However, one of Shinran's great contributions was his assertion that one takes birth in Pure Land and joins the determined class in a

nonretrogressive state the very moment faith in
Amitābha Buddha's primal vows is aroused:

> We say that we abide in the rank of the determined
> class when we meet the Primal Vow of the gift of
> Amida's other-power [tariki] and our minds which re-
> joice at having been granted true faith are assured,
> and when, because we are accepted by him, we have
> the adamantine mind.[5]

This sudden and nonbacksliding nature of Pure Land
faith makes it a true patriarchal faith. From the standpoint of patriarchal faith, it is sudden enlightenment
and nonretrogression that are important whether one
says "I am Buddha," as in the self-power path of
Ch'an, or "I have already been saved by Amitābha
Buddha's primal vows," as in the other-power path of
Pure Land. Thus, it can never be said that Pure Land
doctrine is for "lower level" people and that Ch'an is
for "higher level" people. According to the theory of
patriarchal faith, everyone is a perfect Buddha. Ch'an
Buddhists are perfect Buddhas entering the Ch'an
gate, whereas Pure Land Buddhists are perfect Buddhas entering the Pure Land gate. We can characterize
these two paths in a very general way as follows: Pure
Land is the Buddha's great compassion, and Ch'an is
the Buddha's great wisdom. However, the Buddha's
great compassion and great wisdom must always go
together, as based on a great faith, which is patriarchal
faith. The key message conveyed by the theory of
patriarchal faith is simply this: Do not postpone your
salvation; awaken now. Whether you accomplish this
through other-power or self-power is of secondary concern.

Chapter Twelve
Faith as the Practice
of Compassion

Once patriarchal faith has been aroused, it must be practiced. This does not only include internal practices such as meditation but also involves various kinds of social practices as well. Mahāyāna Buddhism emphasizes that unless faith is practiced through acts of compassion (*karuṇā*) and giving (*dāna*), it is impotent. This is similar to the Christian attitude expressed in the *Letter of James* in the *New Testament*: "Faith apart from works is dead." In the Preface of his translation of the *New Testament* from Latin into German, Martin Luther objected to this passage due to his "faith-only" doctrine. According to Luther, faith, as a gift of God's grace, is sufficient in itself, and requires nothing else to supplement it. In Japan, Shinran's Pure Land doctrine of faith takes a similar position, stating that faith, as a gift of Amida Buddha's Primal Vow, has full saving-power apart from anything else. However, when we say that faith needs good works, we do not intend a "faith plus compassion" formula of salvation. Rather, we mean that compassion is essential to the structure of faith itself as the realization of dependent origination.

Mahāyāna Buddhist faith must also be practiced through nonattachment to *dharmas*, which means that true faith involves total liberation (*mokṣa*). Not forgetting the crucial distinctions between Christian theism and Mahāyāna Buddhism, one may say that the Protestant theologian Schubert M. Ogden clearly expressed this idea of practicing faith through nonattachment and compassion in his book *Faith and Freedom*:

> The conclusion . . . . is that faith in God is indeed the existence of freedom in the twofold sense that it is both existence *in* freedom and existence *for* freedom . . . . It is both the negative freedom *from* all things and the positive freedom *for* all things — to love and serve them by so speaking and acting as to respond to their needs. In this respect, faith is existence *in* freedom, and so a *liberated* existence.[1]

Similarly, in Mahāyāna Buddhism, faith is liberated existence in a state of *mokṣa* or "freedom." It is only when faith is existence in freedom that it may be called patriarchal faith. Moreover, Mahāyāna Buddhist faith is existence in freedom in the two-fold sense of a "negative" freedom *from* all things and a "positive" freedom *for* all things. The negative freedom *from* all things is the practice of faith as nonattachment to all *dharmas*; the positive freedom *for* all things is the practice of faith as compassion (*karuṇā*) and giving (*dāna*). However, in contrast to Ogden's Christian theology of faith, Mahāyāna Buddhist faith does not imply a dualistic "faith in ———" construction but is instead a function of one's own Mind. Nonetheless, for Mahāyāna Buddhism, no less than for Ogden's Protestant theology, the practice of faith is existence in freedom.

One who affirms that "I am Buddha" by arousing patriarchal faith sees everyone else as Buddha too. This has significant implications in terms of one's ethical responsibility toward one's fellow human beings. An enlightened person sees all sentient beings as one with his own body, since Buddha is the dependent origination in which one's body and all others are not separated. Therefore, the suffering of all sentient beings is shared by the Buddhas and Patriarchs. The vows of the Bodhisattva to save all sentient beings originates from this.

Patriarchal faith and Great Compassion (*ta-pei*) can be considered inseparable in Mahāyāna Buddhism. To arouse a patriarchal faith through the production of *bodhicitta* simply means to arouse Great Compassion for all sentient beings; and conversely, to arouse Great Compassion for all sentient beings through the production of *bodhicitta* simply means to arouse patriarchal faith. Both faith and compassion are functions of the One Mind. Therefore, it can be said that the bodhisattva's compassionate motivation to save all sentient beings is identical to the fundamental nature of Mind itself.

The Treatise on the *Perfection of Great Wisdom* (*Ta-chih-tu lun*) describes three different levels of compassion: (1) conditioned by human relationships; (2) conditioned by *dharmas*; and (3) unconditioned. The first compassion is practiced by ordinary people according to their degree of intimacy. The second level of compassion is practiced by bodhisattvas according to their wisdom, whereby sentient beings are perceived as illusory. The third level of compassion in its unconditioned form is that of a Buddha who sees neither the marks of sentient beings nor the marks of *dharma*. Therefore, Buddha's compassion is called *mahā-maitrī-mahākaruṇā* or great mercy and great compassion.[2]

Wŏnhyo gives an excellent description of an enlightened Buddha as "The Greatly Compassionate One Who Saves the World" in his *Haedongso* or *Commentary on Awakening Mahāyāna Faith*:

Buddha . . . . regards all sentient beings as his children

and enters the burning house of the three worlds to save [the people who are] suffering in the fire . . . . The merit of saving the world [consists in] precisely this great compassion. It is compassion which does not distinguish between self and others. It is unconditional compassion. Of all compassions it is the most excellent . . . . Of the myriad virtues associated with the stage of Buddhahood, the Tathāgata uses only great compassion as [his] strength . . . . From this [we] know that all Buddhas use great compassion as [their] power exclusively. Therefore, in order to indicate [what manner of] man [Buddha is, the treatise] calls [him] "the greatly compassionate one."[3]

As Wŏnhyo expresses very clearly in this passage, the defining nature of Great Compassion is that it "does not distinguish between self and others." In the Great Compassion of a bodhisattva, self-benefit and other-benefit are therefore the same. Great Compassion is realized only by returning to the One Mind, the original Mind of non-discrimination. How does one return to the One Mind? By arousing faith in Suchness and the Three Jewels of *Buddha, Dharma* and *Saṃgha,* which in Wŏnhyo's commentary means returning to One Mind with its Three Greatnesses of Essence, Attributes and Functions. Thus, according to Wŏnhyo's understanding, to arouse Mahāyāna Buddhist faith is only to return to One Mind, the bodhisattva's mind of Great Compassion which does not distinguish between self and others.

This kind of Great Compassion is expressed in Mathew 5 (43) of the *New Testament* by the famous words of Jesus:

You have heard that it was said, "You shall love your neighbor and hate your enemy." But I say to you, Love your enemies and pray for those who persecute you, so that you may be sons of your Father who is in heaven, for he makes his sun rise on the evil and on the good, and sends rain on the just and on the unjust. For if you love those who love you, what reward have you? Do not even the tax collectors do the same? And if you salute only your brethren, what more are you doing than others? Do not even the Gentiles do the same? You, therefore, must be perfect, as your heavenly Father is perfect.[4]

In his book *What is Religion?* Keiji Nishitani of the Japanese Kyoto school cites this same passage. As Nishitani points out, the commandment of Jesus to love one's enemies is what Buddhism calls "non-differentiating love beyond enemy and friend." Also, perfection consists in just this kind of non-differentiating love. To hate one's enemies and love one's friends is the position of the ego, what in ancient Greek is termed *eros*, whereas non-differentiating love is the position of "non-ego," or what in Greek is termed *agape*. As Nishitani also says, this non-differentiating love or *agape* which loves the enemy as well as friends consists in "making oneself empty." Here, Nishitani relates this idea of "making oneself empty" through *agape* or non-differentiating love to the Christian idea of *kenōsis*, as well as to Buddhist *anātman* or *muga*, i.e., non-ego or selflessness. Therefore, according to Nishitani's view, non-differentiating love has a profound impersonal or transpersonal aspect, as well as a personal aspect.[5]

It can be said that in Mahāyāna Buddhism there are two traditions: the tradition of *karuṇā* or compassion and the tradition of *prajñā* or wisdom. The *karuṇā* tradition is represented by the vows of Samantabhadra Bodhisattva to save all sentient beings as described in the *Hua-yen ching*, whereas the *prajñā* tradition is represented by the Ch'an tradition, which stresses realization of śūnyatā or emptiness. The *karuṇā* tradition criticizes Ch'an by saying it cannot stop at realizing *śūnyatā*, but must also practice *karuṇā*. However, the Ch'an tradition also criticizes the *karuṇā* tradition, saying that unless there has been a real "revolution of the basis" or *āśraya parāvṛtti*, it does no good to practice so-called compassion, since nothing has been actually changed. One must realize *śūnyatā* or emptiness before compassion can be practiced. The Ch'an tradition argues that practicing *karuṇā* without enlightenment only accumulates more *karma*. Also, they argue that performing good works without realization of *śūnyatā* only reinforces one's ego. Yet, in response, the *karuṇā* tradition says that through the practice of compassion and giving we can realize enlightenment and manifest Buddhahood by eliminating greed, and cutting-off all attachments.

Who is right? The admonition of Ch'an masters not to practice compassion without wisdom cannot be ignored by the *karuṇā* tradition. Therefore, what criterion can we select for the proper method of practicing compassion? Let us say that in order for compassion to be true compassion, i.e., the Great Compassion of Bodhisattva Samantabhadra, it must be practiced on the basis of *faith*. However, this does not mean a doctrinal faith which practices good works in order to realize Buddhahood gradually by accumulating merit, but only a patriarchal faith which affirms one's present Buddhahood and also affirms the present Buddhahood of all other sentient beings as well. Therefore, the criterion for true compassion or *karuṇā* and giving or *dāna* is that it is practiced on the basis of a patriarchal faith.

Part Three
Enlightenment

BODHI (wisdom)

Calligraphy by the eminent Korean monk Kyong-bong (1981).

Chapter Thirteen
Sudden Enlightenment and Gradual Practice

So far, we have discussed the philosophical problems involved in distinguishing between patriarchal faith and doctrinal faith as the basis for the traditional sudden enlightenment and gradual enlightenment, respectively, in East Asian Buddhism. Let us now explore the possibility of a *synthesis* of these two positions through an examination of Chinul's doctrine of *tonochŏmsu*, or "sudden enlightenment and gradual practice." One might naturally assume that such a synthesis would involve a period of gradual practice culminating in an experience of sudden enlightenment. However, in Chinul's synthesis, sudden enlightenment *precedes* gradual practice! According to the theory of patriarchal faith, practice is true practice only after enlightenment is attained. Thus, Chinul asserts that the act of arousing patriarchal faith is the real beginning of one's life of practice and enlightenment.

Chinul derived his theory from Tsung-mi (780–841), a patriarch of both the Hua-yen and Ch'an schools of Buddhism. In his articulation of Sŏn, Chinul argued that all practice *before* enlightenment is only an extension of the dualistic error of discriminating between sentient beings and Buddhas; therefore, it is not true practice. On the other hand, Chinul argued against the doctrine of the Southern school of Ch'an founded by the sixth patriarch Hui-neng (638–713). In the *Platform Sūtra*, Hui-neng states, "Self-awakening by self-nature, and sudden practice with sudden awakening;

[105]

there is nothing gradual in them, so that all methods [of practice] are unnecessary." Here, "sudden" refers to the instantaneous divestment of the mind of its deluded stream of thoughts, and "awakening" is the realization that there is nothing to be attained, that all sentient beings are originally the Buddha. Chinul challenged Hui-neng's theory of "suddenness" and its consequent dictum of "no further practice" because he believed it would cause monks to discontinue practice before attaining final enlightenment.

Although Chinul criticized Hui-neng, he did so without contradicting him. Chinul's doctrine of sudden enlightenment and gradual practice is characterized by two levels of enlightenment: initial insight and ultimate wisdom. Initial insight is defined as "immature" enlightenment. True practice begins only *after* this sudden flash of initial insight. "Suddenness" refers to this initial insight, and "final enlightenment" refers to the second stage of ultimate wisdom. Thus, Chinul simply demonstrated the correct reference of Hui-neng's words. Only after one attains ultimate wisdom is Hui-neng's dictum of "no further practice" valid.

Chinul went beyond Tsung-mi when he directly connected the stage of initial insight with the arousal of a patriarchal faith, which he discovered through reading Li T'ung-hsüan. A critical question must be raised here: If enlightenment is achieved as soon as patriarchal faith is aroused, then why is gradual practice necessary? According to the theory of patriarchal faith, one practices not to attain enlightenment, but to *renew* enlightenment or *reaffirm* one's Buddhahood at every moment, as well as to continually deepen one's initial insight into original Buddha-nature. The theory of sudden enlightenment and gradual practice can perhaps best be understood through the Buddhist idea of *samādhi*. Although this term is used in numerous ways, its general meaning in Buddhism is "a state of trance or deep concentration." This state is a blissful state of nondiscrimination and liberation from all extremes, including pleasure and pain, and attraction and repulsion. In the theory of sudden enlightenment and gradual practice, the initial arousal of patriarchal faith puts one into a state of *samādhi*. Only when one is in *samādhi* can one truly make the claim, "I am Buddha." It is here that we see the radical nature of patriarchal faith in Mahāyāna Buddhism, since an act of faith is equivalent to entering a state of *samādhi*.

However, the achievement of *samādhi* is not the end of one's religious life; it is only the *beginning!* There are many degrees of *samādhi* in Mahāyāna Buddhism. Through gradual practice, the *samādhi* achieved the moment faith is aroused is continually deepened until, in the final stages of the path, full Buddhahood is realized. Therefore, the first *samādhi* trance experienced through the arousal of faith corresponds to what Chinul calls "initial insight" or "sudden enlightenment" and gradually increases through cultivation until one attains ultimate wisdom, or final enlightenment.

Tsung-mi illustrates his theory of sudden enlightenment and gradual practice using the analogy of birth. Sudden enlightenment is simply the birth of a Buddha. The baby is a complete human being, but its capacities differ greatly from those of an adult. Through gradual development, the baby Buddha becomes fully matured.[2] The transformation from nonfaith to faith is therefore a process of becoming *born again*, although this rebirth as a Buddha is only the beginning of one's religious life and not its culmination.

Is the sudden enlightenment described by Tsung-mi and Chinul the same enlightenment of traditional Ch'an Buddhism, or does it involve a serious compromise that understates the meaning of enlightenment? Tsung-mi, for example, was severely criticized by the Lin-chi line of Ch'an Buddhism for his position that gradual practice is required after sudden enlightenment. They condemned him for trivializing the idea of enlightenment. They also argued that his theory was harmful to practitioners since it might cause them to abandon their practice at an initial stage of development. The Lin-chi line of Ch'an argued that, if enlightenment were not total and final, it was not enlightenment at all. This problem is reflected in Tsung-mi's commentary on the *Yüan-chiao ching* or *Sūtra of Perfect Enlightenment*. The *sūtra* states that "every sentient being has perfect enlightenment."[3] In his commentary, however, Tsung-mi made the following major alteration: "Every sentient being has the *potential* for attaining perfect enlightenment" (italics mine). Here, Tsung-mi seemed to be arguing against the tradition of sudden enlightenment and patriarchal faith in favor of the tradition of gradual spiritual development. Consequently, the Lin-chi line of Ch'an Buddhism relentlessly criticized Tsung-mi's alteration of this *sūtra*.[4]

In defense of the theory of sudden enlightenment and gradual practice, it can be argued that those who condemn Tsung-mi's description of enlightenment on the grounds that it is not a true enlightenment, but a mere faith, themselves make the error of seriously understating the meaning of faith in its sense as patriarchal faith. Those who criticize Tsung-mi's theory on the grounds that it encourages people to abandon practice at an immature stage of development ignore the thrust of the theory, which is that sudden enlightenment must be *followed* by gradual practice. Tsung-mi, and later Chinul, tried to cure the disease of gradual practice by means of the medicine of sudden enlightenment and to cure the disease of sudden enlightenment by means of gradual practice. Is this synthesis of the traditions of gradual and sudden enlightenment successful? This is a question for future Buddhist scholarship to resolve. However, one virtue of the system of sudden enlightenment and gradual practice promoted by Tsung-mi and Chinul is that it makes explicit the structure underlying the Hua-yen theory of fifty-two interpenetrating stages. This, however, requires a separate discussion and is the topic of the next chapter.

Chapter Fourteen
Faith and Enlightenment
in the *Hua-yen Sūtra*

Hua-yen Buddhism is based on the idea of *dharmadhātu* (Chinese: *fa chieh*), or the "*dharma* realm." In the *dharma* realm, there is *li shih wu-ai*, or "unobstructed mutual penetration between phenomena and noumena," and *shih shih wu-ai*, or "unobstructed mutual penetration between phenomena and phenomena." The formula *Li shih wu-ai* means that each *dharma* contains the totality, whereas *shih shih wu-ai* means that all *dharmas* mutually contain each other. All *dharmas* interpenetrate because they arise through *pratītyasamutpāda*, or "dependent origination." Since each *dharma* arises through *pratītyasamutpāda*, it has no *svabhāva*, or "self-nature," and therefore mixes through and through with every other *dharma*. As a result of *pratītyasamutpāda* in the *dharma* realm of mutual penetration, "all is in one" and "one is in all." Even though all *dharmas* penetrate each other mutually without obstruction, they still function separately and remain exactly as they are.[1]

The Hua-yen *dharma* realm is often illustrated by the "jewel net of Indra." Here, the universe is likened to a net wherein each intersection has a jewel that reflects the totality (establishing *li shih wu-ai*) as well as all the other jewels (establishing *shih shih wu-ai*) from its own viewpoint in the net. There is thus a mutual reflection among all *dharmas* in the universe, so that one mirrors all and all mirror one.[2]

In Hua-yen, the technical term *yüan ch'i*, or "dependent origination," indicates that all the myriad phenomena in the *dharmadhātu* are interrelated and are therefore interreflecting, interpenetrating, and so on. Because of *yüan ch'i*, each *shih* (particular *dharma*) is identical to *li* (the universal whole). It is this metaphysical theory that *shih* and *li* are mutually penetrating and mutually identical which supports the idea of patriarchal faith that "I am Buddha." Because of the nonobstruction between *li* and *shih*, all things are Buddha. To emphasize this, Hua-yen scholars invented the idea of *hsing-ch'i*, or "nature-origination." Briefly, *hsing-ch'i* describes everything in the *dharmadhātu* as a function (*yung*) of Buddha. The etymological meaning of *hsing-ch'i* is found in the *ju-lai hsing-ch'i* chapter of the *Hua-yen ching*. The earliest appearance of the term occurs in Hui-yüan's *Ta-ch'eng i-chang*, or *On the Meaning of Mahāyāna*, in which it is said that *hsing*, or "nature," in the phrase *hsing-ch'i* refers to "no-change"; "no-change" in turn refers to the *tathāgatagarbha*, i.e., the matrix of Buddha where all things are identical in one Suchness. Later, Chih-yen (602–668), the second patriarch of the Hua-yen school, interpreted the meaning of *hsing-ch'i* as "nonorigination":

> The [doctrine] of nature-origination clarifies the *dharmadhātu* of the One Vehicle. When anything arises through dependent origination, it is originally ultimate being free from artificial practices . . . . Although it is called "origination," such an origination is identical with "non-origination." Non-origination is called nature-origination.[3]

Here, the notion of nature-origination as nonorigination or nonproduction refers to the "uncreated reality" (*wu-sheng fa-jen*) of the *dharmadhātu*. Elsewhere, Chih-yen uses the *t'i-yung*, or "essence–function," construction to show that each *dharma* is a "function" (*yung*) of Buddha (*t'i*), understood as the uncreated reality of nonorigination. As Chih-yen states, "in the term 'nature-origination,' nature means essence (*t'i*) and origination means the appearance or function of essence as the mind-ground." This concept of *hsing-ch'i*, or "nature-origination," was further developed by other traditional Hua-yen patriarchs such as Fa-tsang, Cheng-kuan, and Tsung-mi. However, it was the Hua-yen master Li T'ung-hsüan and later the Korean Sŏn master Chinul who established the *hsing-ch'i* aspect of *yüan ch'i* whereby all *dharma*s are a function (*yung*) of Buddha, who is essence (*t'i*), as the intellectual basis for their idea of patriarchal faith, the affirmation that "I am Buddha." Thus, through the idea of *hsing-ch'i*, we see another dimension of patriarchal faith. Since *hsing-chi* means "origination is nonorigination," all *dharma*s are a function of the uncreated essence, i.e., Buddha. Therefore, an important theme not only in the *Hua-yen ching*, but in many other important Mahāyāna scriptures, such as the *Vimalakīrti Sūtra*, the *Nirvāṇa Sūtra*, and the *Treatise on Awakening Mahāyāna Faith*, is the awakening of a deep faith in uncreated reality, technically termed *anutpattika-dharma-kṣānti*, a "patient endurance of the uncreated realm." Hence, from the standpoint of *hsing-ch'i*, patriarchal faith is faith in uncreated reality or the identity of origination and nonorigination.

Let us now examine how the unobstructed *dharma* world established by the principles of *yüan-ch'i* and *hsing-ch'i* is related to the practical aspects of Hua-yen, i.e., faith, practice, and enlightenment. According to the *Hua-yen ching*, a bodhisattva must pass through

fifty-two stages until he attains marvelous enlightenment. Among these stages are ten faiths, ten abidings,
ten practices, ten returnings, and ten stages, followed
by equal enlightenment and marvelous enlightenment.
According to the traditional interpretation, these
represent the four aspects of the Buddhist religion:
faith, understanding, practice, and enlightenment, as
shown in the following chart:[4]

Faith	(1-10)	Ten faiths
Understanding	(11-20)	Ten abidings
Practice	(21-30)	Ten practices
	(31-40)	Ten returnings
	(41-50)	Ten stages
	(51)	Equal enlightenment
Enlightenment	(52)	Marvelous enlightenment

Because of the mysterious *dharma* world of complete
harmony and nonobstruction, all fifty-two stages in the
career of a bodhisattva interpenetrate without obstruction, although each stage remains distinct. Therefore,
the last stage of marvelous enlightenment is realized at
the first stage of initial faith; the very instant one
awakens one's heart of faith, marvelous enlightenment
is attained. Nonetheless, one must still pass through all
fifty-two stages of faith, understanding, practice, and
enlightenment.

To explain this theory as described in the *Hua-yen
ching*, Tsung-mi and Chinul developed the theory of
sudden enlightenment and gradual practice. On the
basis of Li T'ung-hsüan's insights, Chinul showed that,
in the system of sudden enlightenment and gradual
practice, faith is primary since it represents the first ten
stages of a bodhisattva's path.[5] If sudden enlightenment is reached at the very first stage, then clearly a

correct faith must be awakened, i.e., a patriarchal faith which affirms that "I am *already* Buddha" instead of a doctrinal faith that "I can *become* Buddha." If the traditional notion of doctrinal faith is accepted, the entire structure of the *Hua-yen ching* collapses; for if there is only a doctrinal faith that I can become Buddha by a step-by-step process of gradual development through faith, understanding, practice, and enlightenment, then there is no interpenetration among the fifty-two stages, and the last stage of marvelous enlightenment cannot be contained in the first stage of initial faith. On the other hand, if a true patriarchal faith affirming the identity of sentient beings and Buddha is awakened, Li T'ung-hsüan and Chinul argued, then the initial stage of awakening faith is already marvelous enlightenment. Nonetheless, this realization of Buddhahood is still immature and must be perfected through gradual cultivation, which includes meditation, acts of compassion, giving, being steadfast in one's vows, and developing various *upāya* or "skill-in-means."

Of course, this argument does not in itself prove the truth of patriarchal faith or disprove that of doctrinal faith. After all, it is possible that the Hua-yen theory of fifty-two mutually containing stages is incorrect or, at least, that it is merely an arbitrary scheme. However, my intention here is to demonstrate that the Hua-yen scheme of fifty-two stages does depend on the concept of patriarchal faith, since the first stage of initial faith is identical to the last stage of marvelous enlightenment. The theory of doctrinal faith cannot explain the Hua-yen scheme any more than it can explain the possibility of the Ch'an experience of sudden enlightenment. Thus, I am essentially pointing out the extreme limitations of the theory of doctrinal faith in interpreting East Asian Buddhist ways of thought.

The system of sudden enlightenment and gradual practice developed by Chinul is illustrated by the famous journey of Sudhana described in the thirty-ninth chapter of the *Hua-yen ching*. In order to understand the meaning of Sudhana's journey, we must first familiarize ourselves with the *Hua-yen ching* itself. The *Hua-yen ching* is an enormous text consisting of 80 rolls (in the edition used by Li T'ung-hsüan and Chinul). Although nearly every page refers to the subject of faith, six chapters in particular are known as the chapters on faith: chapter 7, "The Buddha's Names"; chapter 8, "The Four Noble Truths"; chapter 9, "Enlightenment as Light"; chapter 10, "Clarification of the Bodhisattva's Questions"; chapter 11, "The Practice of Purity"; chapter 12, "Hsien-shou Bodhisattva."[6] The different portions of the *sūtra* are delivered to ten assemblies at ten locations, the six chapters on faith being given in the second assembly at the Hall of Universal Light.

Whereas chapters 10, 11, and 12 discuss faith in terms of understanding, practice, and enlightenment, following the standard Hua-yen formula; chapters 7, 8, and 9 explain the Buddha's body, speech, and mind respectively, emphasizing that the Buddha's enlightenment is the content of faith. The key theme in these three chapters is the inseparability of faith and enlightenment. What is the nature of Buddha's enlightenment? This is revealed in the ninth chapter, entitled *Kuang-ming chaio*, "Enlightenment as Light." Here Mañjuśrī, the Buddha of Wisdom, extols the endless, boundless, and immeasurable light emitted by Buddha which illuminates infinite worlds and sentient beings including Mañjuśrī himself. This light gives all sentient beings their faith. Consequently, the actual content of faith is Buddha's light. In *Hua-yen-ching lun*, or *Commentary on the Hua-yen Sūtra*, Li T'ung-hsüan analyzes the opening passages of chapter 9 as follows:

> Why is it named the chapter of Enlightenment as Light? Because of the fact that the *tathāgata* emits the light out of the ring in his feet in the midst of Ten Faiths . . . . Upon being illumined by the light, one awakens one's faith and begins to practice. Hence the chapter of Enlightenment Light. Practitioners follow every light and see all the universe, and the mind seeing them now is also inexhaustible, then becomes identical with the dharma-body and finally enters the first stage of the Ten Abidings.[7]

According to Li T'ung-hsüan, the light emitted by the Buddha awakens one's faith and causes one to practice. In an act of faith, one sees boundless light illuminating the immeasurable universe, and therefore one's mind itself becomes immeasurable. Li T'ung-hsüan then connects the act of faith and the light of Buddha, which is the content of that faith, with entering *samādhi*:

> One who enters the stage of Ten Faiths follows this light of precious colored lamp-clouds and sees both one's inner mind and the universe. If one could have one's mind and the world show no distinction of inside, outside and middle whatsoever, then one would immediately be able to enter into the samādhi of *upāya* . . . . However, if one fails to see the light with precious colors, he cannot achieve the sea of vows made by Samantabhadra and miraculous power of the Tao, and the great functions of all Buddhas will never be accomplished.[8]

Li T'ung-hsüan considers faith, or the experience of Buddha's light in the state of *samādhi*, to be the condition for fulfilling Samantabhadra's sea of vows, as described by the *Hua-yen ching*. These are (1) to honor all Buddhas; (2) to praise all Buddhas; (3) to make extensive offerings to the Buddhas; (4) to repent for all one's sins; (5) to be sympathetically joyful over the merits accumulated by others; (6) to ask the Buddha to revolve the Wheel of the Dharma; (7) to ask the Buddha to stay on living in this world; (8) to learn continually from the life of Buddha; (9) to look after the spiritual welfare of all beings; and (10) to turn all one's merits toward the promotion of good and the suppression of evil.[9] One cannot attain Buddha's enlightenment unless one has fulfilled the ten vows of Samantabhadra, who symbolizes the Buddha's compassion; yet one cannot be steadfast in these vows unless one is firmly rooted in the experience of faith.

There are three different accounts of enlightenment in the *Hua-yen ching*: those of Vairocana Buddha, Bodhisattva Mañjuśrī, and Sudhana. In other words, the *sūtra* describes the enlightenment of a Buddha, a bodhisattva, and an ordinary person. Vairocana Buddha's enlightenment is described on the *bodhi* field under the *bodhi* tree of Maghada, where Gautama Buddha attained realization; Bodhisattva Mañjuśrī's enlightenment is described in the Hall of Universal Light; and Sudhana's is described at Jetavana Monastery. In each case, Gautama Buddha is present but remains silent; he is simply illuminating light throughout the universe and hence is called Vairocana, a Sanskrit term meaning "universally illuminating light." Upon receiving this light, Bodhisattvas Samantabhadra and Mañjuśrī enter *samādhi*, in which state they proceed to give discourses. Why does Gautama Buddha not speak? The Buddha in the *sūtra* is neither historical nor philosophical but experiential. The experience consists of light emitted from the Buddha's side and *samādhi* from the bodhisattva's side. The link between the Buddha's light and the bodhisattva's *samādhi* is faith. Therefore, whenever enlightenment is discussed in the *Hua-yen ching*, it is followed by a discourse on faith. Thus, each of the three stories of enlightenment is also a story of faith. In the case of Vairocana Buddha's enlightenment, faith is represented by Bodhisattva Samantabhadra's great vows and practice; in the second, by Bodhisattva Mañjuśrī's wisdom; and in the third, Sudhana's awakening through Mañjuśrī's instruction. In each case, faith is essentially identical to enlightenment.

Sudhana's journey, which is described in the final chapter of the *Hua-yen ching*, illustrates the entire Hua-yen doctrine of sudden enlightenment and gradual practice as based on a primacy of patriarchal faith. Sudhana is initiated by Mañjuśrī's extollations of the Buddha's light into the stage of initial faith. He then departs on a pilgrimage to fifty-two *kalyāṇamitra*s or "sages." These sages are often said by Buddhist scholars to correspond to the fifty-two stages of a bodhisattva's career described by Hua-yen philosophy. The last sage, Maitreya Buddha, sends Sudhana back to Mañjuśrī. Thus, Mañjuśrī is not only the cause of Sudhana's journey, but also its effect; in other words, he is not only Sudhana's point of departure, but also his final destination. Therefore, Mañjuśrī symbolizes both the level of initial faith and that of final wisdom. For this reason, Hua-yen scholars often consider the most serious theme in the *Hua-yen ching* to be the inseparability of faith and enlightenment.[10]

Even though Sudhana enters *samādhi* at the first state, his journey has just begun. He must still make a pilgrimage to fifty-two stages, in each case entering a deeper level of *samādhi*, until he realizes marvelous enlightenment at the fifty-second stage; yet the fifty-second stage is the same as the first, i.e., Mañjuśrī, the Hua-yen Buddha of faith and wisdom.

How can we intepret the Hua-yen theory of sudden enlightenment and gradual practice as illustrated by Sudhana's journey? In the final analysis, it must be understood in terms of the Hua-yen doctrine on the "degrees" of faith. In the *Hua-yen ching*, faith is divided into ten stages according to its maturity. These ten stages, which were adopted by Fa-tsang from the *She-lun* (or *Mahāyanasamgṛha*) are outlined below:

1. Faith (*hsin*): At the place of entering understanding, pure faith (*śraddhā*) appears. The mind is resolutely determined or wishes to acquire this faith.

2. Heart of mindfulness (*nien*): One practices six kinds of mindfulness, i.e., Buddha, *dharma*, *saṃgha*, *śīla* (precepts), *dāna* (giving), and heaven.

3. Zeal (*ching-chin*): Upon hearing the Mahāyāna doctrine, one practices good behavior diligently and without cessation.

4. *Samādhi* (*ting*): When the doctrine is fully revealed, one's mind is firmly determined and is free of all faults, impulses, conjectures, and discriminations.

5. Wisdom (*hui*): Upon hearing the Mahāyāna doctrine, one contemplates, observes, and completely knows all *dharma*s to be empty by their very nature.

6. Precepts (*chieh*): When one receives a bodhisattva's pure precepts, one's body, speech and mind are purified. One rarely makes mistakes, but if a mistake is made one is regretful and does not repeat it.

7. Returning (*hui-hsiang*): All good roots that have

[119]

been cultivated are returned to [i.e., shared with] all sentient beings.

8. Protecting *dharma* (*hu-fa*): One protects one's heart from defilements and further cultivates the protection of silence, the protection of wisdom, the protection of mindfulness, and the protection of quiescence.

9. Renunciation (*she*): One does not pay attention to one's own body and wealth. Therefore, the bodhisattva is able to renounce all attachments.

10. Vows (*yüan*): One practices various pure vows without cessation.[11]

According to the Hua-yen doctrine of ten faiths, the experience of faith is not static but has various "degrees" of intensity. The initial awakening of faith, which is the result of seeing Buddha's light, produces a state of *samādhi*, as described by Li T'ung-hsüan; this *samādhi* then deepens throughout the ten stages of development. Chinul, Li T'ung-hsüan, and many other commentators on the *Hua-yen ching* say that the ten faiths in themselves represent a complete series that embraces the entire scheme of the fifty-two stages. Accordingly, the eleventh stage in the career of a bodhisattva, which is the first abode, i.e., the first stage of *shih chu*, or the "ten abidings," corresponds to the fifty-second stage of marvelous enlightenment. In other terms, it represents the transformation of *hsin-hsin*, "the mind of faith," into *fa-hsin*, "the mind of wisdom," which is the perfection of faith, as described in the *Treatise on Awakening Mahāyāna Faith*. Consequently, the first stage (of initial faith), the eleventh stage (the first abode), and the fifty-second stage (marvelous enlightenment) are all correlates. In his summary of Li T'ung-hsüan's commentary on the *Hua-yen ching*, Chinul writes:

I have carefully examined that which was illumned by this commentary. It says that in the Three Vehicles, ultimate enlightenment is reached only after one passes through the ten stages. Yet, according to the One Vehicle [of Hua-yen], the Buddha's enlightenment is attained in the very first stage of the ten faiths. In terms of stages, enlightenment is realized in the first stage of the Ten Abodes [i.e., the eleventh stage]. If one enters into the first stage of faith, he then reaches the first abode as well without any effort. If he reaches the first abode, he naturally reaches the ultimate stage [marvelous enlightenment, or the fifty-second stage]. This being the case, what is most essentially required for an ordinary person in the ocean of suffering is the first awakening of correct faith.[12]

Understood in this way, the entire scheme of fifty-two stages described by the *Hua-yen ching* simply represents the content of initial faith. As soon as faith is aroused, all fifty-two stages are embraced, since they are the true content of that faith. However, these fifty-two stages must now be articulated, as it were, through gradual practice. The first stage of initial faith produces *samādhi*, which must be deepened many degrees, until the eleventh stage, corresponding to marvelous enlightenment at the fifty-second stage, is realized. Nonetheless, all of the bodhisattva's immeasurable compassion, vows, practices, and states of *samādhi* are simply different aspects of a single act of initial faith. Faith is the bodhisattva's point of departure, the force sustaining him throughout his career, and the culimination of that career in marvelous enlightenment, which is the perfection of faith. Therefore, it can be said that, in Hua-yen Buddhism, faith, in its sense as patriarchal faith, is the beginning, middle, and end of the religious process, which means that faith, practice, and enlightenment are in essence the same.

In summary, according to Hua-yen, the content of faith is simply the whole *dharmadhātu* of mutual penetration where all is one and one is all. This means that faith is in essence the realization of nonduality, i.e., emptiness or Suchness. To arouse faith, in its sense as patriarchal faith, is to realize one's identity with the *dharma* realm of dependent origination. A famous poem in East Asian Buddhism, "Song of Faith" (*hsin-hsin ming*), which is traditionally attributed to Seng-t'san, the third patriarch of the Ch'an school, succinctly conveys the Hua-yen idea of patriarchal faith:

The Essence [of reality] is beyond time and space,
For in one instant is ten thousand years;
Beyond existence and non-existence
It is manifest everywhere in all the ten quarters.

Infinitely small things are identical to the large
For all external conditions are gone
Infinitely large things are identical to the small
For objective limits are forgotten. . . . .

One in All
All in One
If this is realized
One attains perfection

Faith is non-duality
Non-duality is faith.
Here words fail.
For it is beyond past, present and future.[13]

Chapter Fifteen
Kkaech'im: The Experience of Brokenness

In China, the experience of enlightenment is expressed by such terms as *wu, chiao,* and *chien-sheng.* In Japan, it is expressed by *kensho* and *satori.* In colloquial Korean vocabulary, enlightenment is denoted by *kkaech'im.* This term is ultimately derived from the ancient verbal root *kkaeda,* which means "to awaken," "to become sober," "to become aware," "to be hatched or born anew," "to return to life," "to wake up," or "to break." This has two major derivatives: *kkaejida,* "having been broken" or "breakage," and *kkaech'ida,* "to awaken." The noun form of the latter, *kkaech'im,* is the Korean word for "enlightenment." Of special interest here is the relation between *kkaech'im* as "enlightenment" and *kkaejim* as "brokenness." Now, the Korean concept of enlightenment assumes the meaning of "breaking," "brokenness," "breakage," "to break," or "breakthrough."[1]

What is it that must be "broken" in the enlightenment experience? It is one's dualistic intellectual framework and attachment to ego. How does this breakage occur? To answer this question we must again refer to the dynamics of faith activating the process of questioning meditation in *kung-an* practice. Korean Sŏn or Ch'an Buddhism is unique in that it is almost entirely dominated by *kung-an* (Korean: *kong'an*) practice, also termed *kanhwa* or *hwadu* meditation in Korea. Consequently, we can expect the Korean insight into the enlightenment experience as *kaech'im,* or "brokenness," to reflect the dynamics of *kong'an* practice as outlined in chapter 9 on questioning meditation and the dynamics of faith.[2]

It will be recalled that, in the dynamic model of faith operating in the questioning meditation of *kung-an* practice, there are "three essentials": (1) a deep faith that "I am Buddha"; (2) a doubt negating this faith, or a confession that "I am an ignorant sentient being"; and (3) an unbroken process of inward questioning, which represents the dialectic struggle between the two poles of faith and doubt or affirmation and negation.

At the level of actual practice in the Lin-chi tradition of Sŏn or Ch'an Buddhism, this dynamic struggle can be related to the tension arising between reverence (for one's teacher or the scriptures) and honesty (about one's present level of attainment). Because of reverence for my teacher or the words of Buddha recorded in the scriptures, I have deep faith that I am Buddha; yet, because of my honesty concerning my present level of attainment, I must acknowledge that, in truth, I am an ignorant sentient being. To transform this intense existential struggle into a positive form of practice, the teacher prescribes a *kung-an* meditation so that this hidden conflict will become an open one. One might say that one's deep faith is like a burning flame and that one's doubt is a fuel for the flame. The *kung-an* prescribed by the teacher is like dynamite, and the questioning practice itself is a great explosion that takes place when all the volatile ingredients are combined. Hence, it is the *kung-an* that ignites the explosive enlightenment experience of *kkaech'im* or "brokenness."

On a psychological level, one can say that the conflict between the affirmation that "I am Buddha" and the negation that "I am an ignorant sentient being," as well as between one's reverence for the teacher's words and honesty concerning one's present level of attainment, generates a kind of identity crisis. To resolve this crisis, the Sŏn master gives the struggling student a *kung-an* such as "Why *wu*?", "What is mind?" or "What is the sound of one hand clapping?" This intensifies the conflict until at last the student's dualistic framework and ego structure are completely "broken."

Why is the enlightenment experience of *kkaech'im*, or "brokenness" so difficult to achieve? In order for this breaking to occur, the polar conflict between affirmation and negation, faith and doubt, or "I am Buddha" and "I am an ignorant sentient being," must be brought to its extreme. There must be 100 percent reverence for the teacher's words and 100 percent honesty toward one's own degree of attainment. If even 1 percent of either reverence and honesty or faith and doubt is lacking, then although the polar tension might be great, the breaking experience of *kkaech'im* cannot occur, since the extreme limit of these poles has not yet been reached. If only faith and reverence are present one's practice declines into blind fundamentalism, whereas if only doubt and honesty are present one's practice declines into negativism or skepticism. It is therefore only with complete reverence and honesty or faith and doubt that the dynamics of questioning meditation can successfully ignite the explosive enlightenment experience of *kkaech'im*, which as Wumen wrote, is simply the casting away of discriminating mind," in "a moment of yes-and-no."[3]

Chapter Sixteen
Revolution of the Basis

An act of patriarchal faith, as a courageous affirmation of one's own original Buddhahood, involves a
radical transformation of consciousness. In Christianity, the act of faith is said to involve an experience of
conversio or "conversion," such as was so vividly por-
trayed in the lives of St. Paul and St. Augustine.
Mahāyāna Buddhist patriarchal faith may also be said
to involve a type of *conversio*, although in its Buddhist
sense, *conversio* does not mean receiving through grace
a deep commitment to God, Christ, or the Holy Trin-
ity, but an awakening to the nature of one's own Mind.
Again, the Mahāyāna Buddhist experience of *conversio* through faith may be understood as "taking refuge"
in *triratna*, the Three Jewels of Buddha, Dharma and
Saṃgha. However, according to Wŏnhyo's interpretation, awakening faith as taking refuge in *triratna* or
the Three Jewels means simply returning to the One
Mind, with its Three Greatnesses of Essence, Attributes
and Functions (*t'i, hsiang* and *yung*).[1]

In Mahāyāna Buddhism, this *conversio* or revolution
of consciousness which occurs through arousing faith
may be described through the traditional Yogācāra
doctrine of *āśraya parāvṛtti* or "revolution of the
basis." *Āśraya parāvṛtti* has been known as a major
doctrine discussing the enlightenment experience in
Buddhism. Yogācāra is usually referred to as the school
of *vijñāna mātratā* or "Consciousness-only," and involves a doctrine of eight consciousnesses. These include the five sense consciousnesses, mind-conscious-
ness, ego-consciousness, and finally the eighth con-

sciousness, termed *ālaya vijñāna* or the storehouse consciousness. *Vāsanās* or habit-energies from the beginningless past are accumulated in this storehouse consciousness and lead to the projection of the seven lower consciousnesses. These seven lower consciousnesses create an egoistic discrimination of an external world based on the dualism of subject and object, which in turn leads to attachment, suffering, and the endless round of transmigration.

Āśraya parāvṛtti or revolution of the basis indicates a sudden revulsion, turning, or re-turning of the *ālaya vijñāna* back into its original state of purity. That is to say, through *āśraya parāvṛtti*, the seven lower consciousnesses which create the egoistic discrimination of an external world based on the dualism of subject and object are eliminated, as are the habit-energies (*vāsanās*) or habitual perfumings of the storehouse consciousness, so that the Mind returns to its original condition of non-attachment, non-discrimination and non-duality.[2]

The Yogācāra doctrine of consciousness-only holds that there is no "object" external to a "subject" in the sense that ordinary people assume. But again their real purpose of denying the existence of objects is also to deny the existence of subjects. This may sound like a form of nihilism. However, we should not fail to grasp the main point of the Yōgācara doctrine, which is to explain the true relationships between subject and object. This relationship is explained by such terms as *kārana* or creator and *kārya* or created. The terms *kārana* and *kārya* can be translated in various ways such as maker and the made, doer and what is done, seer and the seen, hearer and the heard, and so on. According to Yogācāra doctrine, the true relationship between these seeming opposites of *kārana* and *kārya* or creator and created is one of simultaneity. For example, in the event of one's seeing a flower, in which the one who sees is *kāraṇa* or creator whereas the flower seen is *kārya* or created, both *kāraṇa* and *kārya* occur simultaneously, yet the two are not identical.

The second important feature of this relationship is that *kāraṇa* and *kārya* are interchangeable. That is to say that in the event of one's seeing a flower, the flower seen can also be a *kāraṇa* whereas the one who sees the flower can be a *kārya*. In other words, human consciousness is not always fixed as *kāraṇa*: it can also be a *kārya*. When our consciousness functions as a *kāraṇa*, all the *kāryas* are described as being produced (*utpāda*) by our consciousness whereas when all the *kāryas* are transformed into *kāraṇa* and our consciousness becomes *kārya*, our consciousness is described as being perfumed (*vāsanā*) by *kāraṇa* This two-way relationship may be shown as in the following diagram:

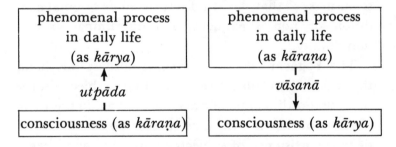

The key point of this diagram is to show that consciousness is both *kāraṇa* and *kārya*, and at the same time, the phenomenal process is both *kāraṇa* and *kārya*. Thus, the relationship between *kāraṇa* and *kārya* may be characterized by the two notions of simultaneity and interchangeability.

The word *kāraṇa* is sometimes also taken as "cause" whereas *kārya* is "effect." Hence, the *āśrya parāvṛtti* or transformation of the basis occurring through the arousal of faith, results in the realization of the interchangeability of *kāraṇa* and *kārya* or cause and effect. *Kāraṇa* is not always fixed as *kāraṇa*, and *kārya* is not always fixed as *kārya*. *Kāraṇa* functions as *kārya* as well as it works as *kāraṇa*. How is it possible? It is solely because of the original structure of consciousness which is related to everything through *pratītyasamutpāda*.[3]

The Yogācāra theory of human consciousness elaborates the dependent nature of everything. In terms of human perception, there is nothing which is not influenced by human consciousness, and also, there is nothing which does not influence human consciousness. Therefore, the dependent nature seen in this relationship between internal consciousness and phenomenal process in the external world is not static but dynamic. This structure of human consciousness is seen in everybody whether one is enlightened or not. If our present consciousness functions as a *kāraṇa* or cause which produces the phenomenal process as its *kārya* or effect, an endless cycle of transmigration (*saṃsāra*) is established. Since one is ignorant, his consciousness projects a delusory phenomenon; the delusory phenomenon in turn influences by perfuming his ignorant consciousness. This is what is called transmigration.

What will bring about a breakthrough into this cycle? It is for this purpose that the Yogācāra school introduced the *trisvabhāva* or "three-natures" theory. The three-natures are: (1) the dependent nature (*paratantra-svabhāva*); (2) the discriminated nature (*parikalpita-svabhāva*); (3) the perfected nature (*pariniṣpanna-svabhāva*). These three natures are not three components of the world. Rather, they are three ways of seeing one world. *Paratantra* is the world of dependent coorigination and is the basis for both *parikalpita* or the discriminated nature of ignorant sentient beings as well as *pariniṣpanna* or the perfected nature of enlightened Buddhas.

Ordinary sentient beings who are not aware of the dependent nature of the world are attached to discriminated nature. This is the dualistic world of unenlightened people in which subject and object as well as *kāraṇa* and *kārya* are falsely discriminated. If one can eliminate the discrimination completely and see the dependent nature of all things, then the discriminated nature is transformed into perfected nature. Therefore, *pariniṣpanna* or perfected nature is nothing but the actual realization of *paratantra* or dependent nature. The reason Yogācāra masters added the perfected nature to the dependent nature in their scheme is to ensure the completion of *yogācāra*, i.e., the practice of yoga. In other words, it is to overcome the seemingly theoretical dimension of dependent nature and also to discourage immature practitioners from falsely claiming the completion of their practice.

Therefore, we can say that both the discriminated nature and the perfected nature do not exist apart from the dependent nature. Both the possibility of unenlightened people's false discrimination and their transformation into perfected nature are originated from the dependent nature, i.e., the world of *pratītyasamutpāda* or dependent origination. There is a vast gap between the discriminated nature and the perfected nature. However disconnected these two natures may seem, the gap is created by the discriminative acts of unenlightened sentient beings, and is therefore illusory. Thus, the removal of this illusory gap created by the artificial distinctions of discriminated nature shifts us to the world of perfected nature where dependent origination functions properly.

In a word, this shift from discriminated nature to perfected nature and the awakening to oneself as dependent nature is *āśraya parāvṛtti*, "revolution of the basis." The eminent Japanese scholar Gadjin Nagao has especially emphasized the centrality of *āśraya parāvṛtti* in the Yogācāra system. Nagao explains his concept of *āśraya parāvṛtti* as follows:[4]

Āśraya parāvṛtti means, as the word indicates, the basis on which one relies revolves and turns into a different basis (or non-basis); the ground itself on which one stands overturns, revealing a new world, illuminated by a new light. There is the anxiety of one's foothold being fundamentally challenged — the anxiety that it might collapse and disappear, meaning death. But through this death, there is the possibility of the same basic structure coming to life again by being illuminated with a new light. This is not simply the renovation of the mind . . . . it is the conversion and the transmutation of one's whole existence. For instance, if we imagine a magnetic field flowing through a man's being then the *āśraya parāvṛtti* would be the flow of this magnetic field flowing in the opposite direction from its usual flow.

In Yogācāra philosophy, this revolution of the basis is also related to the doctrine of *vijñāna-pariṇāma* or "transformation of consciousness." In both *āśraya paravṛtti* or revolution of the basis and *vijñāna pariṇāma* as transformation of consciousness, the key idea is found in the theory of dependent origination. When the theory of dependent origination is applied to the relationship between internal consciousness and external phenomena, there comes the theory of *vijñāna-pariṇāma* showing the simultaneous interchangeability between human consciousness and the world as a phenomenon; whereas when the theory of dependent origination is applied to the relationship between the discriminated nature and perfected nature, there comes the *āśraya parāvṛtti* doctrine showing how to shift from the world of false distinctions to the world of *pratītyasamutpāda*.

[131]

The arousal of patriarchal faith as well as the attainment of sudden enlightenment are both possible due to the theory of dependent origination. Sentient beings and enlightened Buddhas have in fact never truly been separated from the world of dependent origination even for a single moment, but only seem disconnected due to the artificial distinctions of discriminated nature. Yet, by breaking our attachments to discriminated nature, we can realize instantly the perfect world of dependent origination, which all along has underlied the former as its real basis. And this sudden shift from discriminated nature to perfect nature is *āsraya parāvṛtti*, transformation of the basis. What is the dynamic power which activates *āsraya parāvṛtti*? It is the arousal of patriarch faith, which affirms the identity of sentient beings with Buddha. Therefore, one can say that the Yogācāra doctrine of *āsraya parāvṛtti* or revolution of the basis, and its associated doctrines of three-natures, transformation of consciousness, and the theory of eight consciousnesses, altogether provide us with an excellent description of the actual dynamics of change involved in an act of patriarchal faith. Now, in the following chapter, it remains to be seen how the *āsraya parāvṛtti* or revolution of the basis which occurs through arousing faith involves what the Ch'an tradition regards as the "cutting-off of all streams" in the experience of total *brokenness*.

Chapter Seventeen
The Three Gates

In our discussion of faith, "right faith" (*cheng-hsin*) was identified as patriarchal faith, the affirmation that "I am Buddha." The criterion for establishing faith as patriarchal was shown to be its "unretrogressive" or "nonbacksliding" nature. This nonbacksliding faith (*pu-t'ui hsin*) is that acquired by the family (*gotra*) of *niyati rāśi*, the "determined class," as stated by the *Ta-ch'eng ch'i-hsin lun* or *Treatise on Awakening Mahāyāna Faith*. Next, in our discussion of practice as the function (*yung*) of patriarchal faith which is understood as essence (*t'i*), the criterion for "right practice" was identified as *ning-chu pi-kuan*, or "abiding firmly in faith through nondual meditation like a wall." Now, we must ask, What is the criterion for "right enlightenment"? From the viewpoint of the Lin-chi tradition of *kung-an* Ch'an, the criterion is *san-kuan*, or the "three gates," which can also be called the "three tests" or "three passes."

The fourteenth-century Korean Sŏn master of the Koryŏ dynasty, Naong, who was the founder of the Lin-chi tradition of *kung-an* Sŏn in Korea, introduces the criterion of *san-kuan* (Korean: *samgwan*). In order for a practitioner of *kung-an* questioning meditation to have his experience of enlightenment as *kkaech'im*, or "brokenness," fully certified by the Ch'an master, the criterion of *san-kuan* must be fulfilled.[1] This means that the practioner must persist in his process of inward questioning without interruption and with full one-pointed concentration throughout the three states of wakefulness, dream, and deep sleep.

In the Lin-chi tradition, the experience that one has during the questioning meditation, no matter how wonderful, is not as important as one's persistence: One must keep questioning, without distraction and without interruption. Therefore, just as the criterion for "right faith" is *pu-t'ui*, or "nonbacksliding," and the criterion for "right practice" is *ning-chu*, or "firmly abiding," the criterion for "right enlightenment" as determined by *san-kuan* or the "three gates" is technically termed, in Ch'an literature, *pu-tuan*, or "noninterruption." This is the stage that the *kung-an* tradition of Ch'an Buddhism calls *hua-t'ou shun-shu*, which means "The *kung-an* has completely matured," as well as *i-t'uan tu-lu*, "only a stream of questioning is manifested." However, in the final analysis, since right faith, right practice, and right enlightenment form an indivisible unity in Buddhism, they ultimately all have the same criterion, namely, *pu-erh*, or "nonduality."[2]

To pass the first of the three gates means to continue one's inward questioning of the *kung-an* without interruption throughout one's waking hours, whether one is walking, standing, sitting, or reclining. To pass the second gate means to continue with one's questioning during one's dreams, regardless of the images that appear before the mind's eye. Finally, to pass the third gate means to continue one's questioning of the *kung-an* even in the state of deep sleep, which is also the state of coma; ultimately, it means that one can hold the *kung-an* even through death. In Ch'an Buddhism this passing of the third gate by holding one's *kung-an* throughout deep sleep, coma, and death is also called living in the *ālaya vijñāna*, or "storehouse consciousness." This is the eighth final consciousness, which is the stream of *vāsanā*s, or "habit-energies," that continues even after death. However, Ch'an masters warn practitioners not to abide in the enjoyment of the storehouse consciousness, which they term *ti-pa mo-chieh*, or the "eighth devil world," but to be completely detached from this state so that total *kkaech'im* is possible.[3]

A story about Ta-hui (1083–1163), the most famous Ch'an master of the Lin-chi line, perhaps best illustrates the level of attainment one must achieve in order to meet the criterion of *san-kuan* and thus have one's enlightened state of *kkaech'im* certified by a Ch'an teacher.[4] Ta-hui, who is famous for burning his teacher's book, *The Blue Cliff Records* (now known as Ta-hui's immortal commentary), as well as for popularizing the method of *kung-an* questioning meditation, once claimed to have attained perfect enlightenment. His teacher, Yüan-wu, insisted that he had not attained true enlightenment. Ta-hui thought to himself, "This old fool isn't really enlightened after all, since he doesn't recognize my own supreme enlightenment." He then decided to leave Yüan-wu and go off on his own. Yüan-wu warned Ta-hui that if he left he would soon become afflicted with a terminal illness and would realize for himself that he had not achieved true enlightenment. "This poor old fool is very stupid indeed!" Ta-hui said to himself, and left. He traveled throughout the land, proclaiming his supreme enlightenment and meanwhile gathering a large following. Then one day he fell seriously ill, just as his old master Yüan-wu had predicted, and finally fell into a coma. During this time, Ta-hui sank into a deep unconscious state and failed to hold his *kung-an*. Upon returning to consciousness, Ta-hui, who was still seriously ill, realized that in truth he had not yet attained real enlightenment, since the *kung-an* questioning meditation had been stopped by the coma. This meant that he had not passed the third gate of *san-kuan*. He then sincerely prayed to all the Buddhas of the ten directions to heal him, promising to return to his teacher and practice his devotion with all his strength if only he would be allowed to recover his health. Miraculously, Ta-hui recovered, and keeping his promise, he immediately returned to his teacher and resumed his practices as though a mere novice. Eventually, Ta-hui did attain the supreme enlightenment, and this was instantly recognized by Yüan-wu. Nonetheless, Ta-hui continued his devotion as though still a beginner, all the while doing his humble monastic duties and kitchen chores and never claiming enlightenment to anyone. Then one day, Yüan-wu asked Ta-hui to come for a walk in the forest. At one point, Yüan-wu unexpectedly pushed Ta-hui into a whirlpool rotating wildly beneath a waterfall. At the last possible moment, when Ta-hui was close to death, Yüan-wu handed him his walking staff and pulled him up until only his mouth and ears cleared the water's surface, allowing him to gasp for air. At this moment, Yüan-wu shouted out a *kung-an* question, whereupon Ta-hui instantly responded as though sitting peacefully in a quiet room. According to the legend, Yüan-wu submerged Ta-hui in the whirlpool to the point of drowning many times before he finally allowed him to climb back onto dry land. It was only then that Yüan-wu certified Ta-hui's attainment of supreme enlightenment, since he had now passed the third gate, beyond sleep, coma, and even death itself.

Conclusion

In this book I have argued that right practice and right enlightenment are determined by right faith. I have also tried to demonstrate that faith represents a missing link in modern Buddhist scholarship. The gap between understanding and practice is overcome by arousing right faith, since it is faith that activates practice and enlightenment. Thus, faith has a primary role in the practical and soteriological aspects of Buddhism. Following the Korean monk Chinul and the Lin-chi line of *Kung-an* Ch'an, I have attempted to show that in Buddhism right faith is a patriarchal faith that "I am Buddha" rather than the more traditional doctrinal faith that "I can become Buddha." Whereas doctrinal faith forms the basis of gradual enlightenment, patriarchal faith is the basis of sudden enlightenment. Is sudden enlightenment in fact possible? My conclusion is that, if sudden enlightenment is possible, it is possible only on the basis of patriarchal faith, which affirms the identity of sentient beings with Buddha. For the sake of my arguments, I have defined "Buddha" in terms of such Buddhist philosophical concepts as emptiness (*śūnyatā*) and dependent origination (*pratītyasamutpāda*). Thus, if all *dharmas* are empty, since they arise from dependent origination, then all *dharmas* are originally Buddha; this serves as an ontological basis for patriarchal faith, or the affirmation that "I am Buddha."

What is the *criterion* for right faith? Following the *Ta-ch'eng ch'i-hsin lun*, or *Treatise on Awakening Mahāyāna Faith*, and the East Asian tradition of Mahāyāna Buddhism in general, I have suggested that right faith is a nonbacksliding or unretrogressive faith (*pu-t'ui hsin*) acquired by members of *niyata rāśi*, or the "determined class." Is a nonbacksliding faith possible? Christian theism claims that faith is a function of reason and will. Since reason can assent to falsehoods and the will is capable of relapse, faith is always subject to backsliding. Moreover, if faith is a gift of God's almighty grace, one can never be sure of having a nonbacksliding faith, since it comes from an external source. I have pointed out that Buddhist doctrinal faith is also a function of will and reason, since it depends on gradual practice, which involves human effort and belief. Patriarchal faith, on the other hand, is not a function of reason and will, but of emptiness and dependent origination, and is thus ontologically grounded in the nature of reality itself. As such, patriarchal faith is not subject to backsliding. Moreover, I have classified the faith obtained as a gift of God's grace as a form of "other-power" faith; the faith of Ch'an and Hua-yen Buddhism, however, is a "self-power" faith, since it is regarded as a function (*yung*) of One Mind, i.e., the Mind of nonthought and nondiscrimination, which is understood as essence (*t'i*). Furthermore, since patriarchal faith is a function of One Mind, it cannot fall back because in a mind free of thought, there is no discrimination between sentient beings and Buddha, and thus there is no one to fall back and no place to fall back to.[1]

Finally, I have supported the claim that a true nonbacksliding faith is possible by the Buddhist idea of *āśraya parāvṛtti*, or "revolution of the basis." Here, the act of arousing a patriarchal faith involves a complex process of "revolution of the basis," bringing about not only a sudden enlightenment, but also an *irreversible* enlightenment. This revolution of the basis is associated with the shift from *hsin-hsin*, the "mind of faith," to *fa-hsin*, the "mind of wisdom." Whereas the

[138]

way from *hsin-hsin* to *fa-hsin* is always open, the way from *fa-hsin* to *hsin-hsin* is permanently closed. Thus, an enlightened Buddha cannot fall back to the level of a sentient being any more than a butterfly can turn back into a caterpillar or a frog into a tadpole. In other words, an act of arousing patriarchal faith brings about a radical *metamorphosis*, an internal change in the structure of one's consciousness that is irreversible, unretrogressive, and nonbacksliding.

In order to explain the relationship between doctrinal faith and patriarchal faith, I have related them to the Mahāyāna Buddhist theory of "two truths." Whereas doctrinal faith is related to *samvṛti satya*, or "relative truth," patriarchal faith is related to *paramārtha satya*, or "absolute truth." Although certain Mahāyāna texts support the doctrinal faith that "I can become Buddha" through gradual cultivation, this is to be understood as an *upāya*, or "skill-in-means," whereby the teachings of the Buddha must be adjusted to suit the various capacities of students who, as a result of their attachment to a dualistic framework, cannot yet accept that they are already Buddha. However, doctrinal faith, valid at the level of *samvṛti satya* as an *upāya*, must ultimately be transformed into nonbacksliding patriarchal faith at the level of *paramārtha satya* if enlightenment is ever to be attained.

One characteristic of Mahāyāna Buddhist faith, it is claimed, is that it must manifest itself in practice. Faith is practiced not only through meditation and internal discipline, but also through moral practices such as compassion and giving. Following Ogden, I have argued that the practice of faith involves *freedom*, i.e., *mokṣa*, or "liberation," including both a "negative" freedom *from* all things through nonattachment and a "positive" freedom *for* all things through compassion. Therefore, the life of faith is the life of freedom.

However, Buddhist practice can be performed on the basis of either doctrinal faith or patriarchal faith. Whereas doctrinal faith is regarded as a preliminary to practice and enlightenment, patriarchal faith *is* practice, *is* enlightenment. Thus, doctrinal faith involves a process of gradual cultivation that passes through faith, understanding, practice, and enlightenment, whereas patriarchal faith produces "sudden enlightenment through sudden practice" (*tun-wu tun-hsiu*), to use the phrase of the sixth patriarch Hui-neng.

The school of sudden enlightenment argues that enlightenment can never be attained by gradual practice, since such practice is merely an extension of a dualistic way of thinking that distinguishes sentient beings from Buddhas. One who believes that enlightenment can be attained by gradual practice therefore puts a gap between oneself and Buddha, which one tries to bridge through practice. The school of sudden enlightenment claims that this gap is not a real entity in the external world, but is merely a discrimination of the mind and can be removed only when one's mind ceases to discriminate. In other words, the gap is an illusion, and this illusion can be dispelled only by the realization that it is an illusion. The school of gradual enlightenment likens the mind to a mirror which must be polished so that dust (i.e., defilement) does not accumulate on it. However, the school of sudden enlightenment asks, "Since mind is originally empty and unsubstantial, where can dust alight?" Hence, the latter school accuses the former of substantializing the mind, i.e., giving it self-nature (*svabhāva*), and then using an analogy that corresponds to it in order to justify the system of gradual cultivation.

Finally, in the Mahāyāna Buddhist tradition of East Asia, the concept of faith is based on a nondual *t'i-yung*, or "essence-function," formula rather than the dualistic *neng-so*, or "subject-object," formula, which is expressed in the "faith in ———" construction. Consequently, in Mahāyāna Buddhism, faith does not require an object, but is instead a natural function (*yung*) of one's own Mind, which is *t'i*, or "essence." However, the doctrinal faith of the school of gradual enlightenment, or the conviction that "I can *become* Buddha," establishes a dualism and therefore objectifies Buddha. Thus, it merely reintroduces the subject-object dichotomy in other terms. It can therefore be claimed that the gradualist position presupposes a dualistic subject-object structure that is alien to the key principle of East Asian Mahāyāna Buddhism, which is nonduality.

One of the basic points that I have attempted to establish is that patriarchal faith is the foundation of Hua-yen Buddhism. According to Hua-yen, since the fifty-two stages in the career of a bodhisattva are mutually containing, the first stage of initial faith is identical to the last stage of marvelous enlightenment. If the first stage is identical to the last, then such a faith is by definition a patriarchal faith. That is, if the fifty-two stages of bodhisattva's career began with only a doctrinal faith, then the mutual containment of the fifty-two stages as well as the identity between the first and last stages would be denied; consequently, the entire structure of the Hua-yen doctrine would collapse. Therefore, to explain the structure of Hua-yen I have shown that sudden enlightenment must *precede* gradual practice, as suggested by Tsung-mi and Chinul.

Moreover, at the level of practice, patriarchal faith is not static, a mere affirmation, but has a *dynamic* nature involving a kind of dialectic tension or polar struggle between affirmation and negation or faith and

doubt, i.e., a dynamic conflict between the two extremes of "I am Buddha" and "I am an ignorant sentient being." In order to resolve this conflict, Ch'an
masters of the Lin-chi line invented the *kung-an*
(Japanese: *kōan*,) meditation. As analyzed in terms of
three essentials of the Ch'an master Kao-feng, *kung-an*
meditation involves an element of great faith and an
element of great doubt, which are resolved in an act of
inward questioning, i.e., *kung-an* meditation. In the
context of Ch'an Buddhism, "great doubt" (*ta-i*) does
not mean the methodological doubt of Descartes or the
skeptical doubt of Hume, but an unbroken inward
questioning. In this context, then, I have related
Mahāyāna Buddhist patriarchal faith to the dynamic
model of faith described by existentialist Sören
Kierkegaard as well as the Christian theologian Paul
Tillich, who argued that doubt is implicit in each act of
faith. Tillich's faith means "ultimate concern," and his
doubt is a profound "existential" doubt; thus, the
stronger one's doubt, the deeper is one's faith, or
ultimate concern. In Ch'an *kung-an* practice, the
dialectic struggle between faith and doubt, affirmation
and negation, or "I am Buddha" and "I am an ignorant sentient being" is brought to its limit, until at
last it explodes, so to speak, in the experience of great
enlightenment, which in the *kung-an* (Korean:
kong'an) tradition of Korean Ch'an or Sŏn is termed
kkaech'im, "brokenness." This experience of complete
brokenness represents the shattering of one's dualistic
framework by which one discriminates between
enlightenment and nonenlightenment or Buddha and
sentient beings. Therefore, in the enlightenment experience of brokenness, one shifts from the
discriminated world of ignorant sentient beings to the
nondiscriminated world of enlightened Buddhas.

What is the criterion for right enlightenment as
kkaech'im? Just as the criterion for right faith is that it

be nonbacksliding (*pu-t'ui*) or irreversible, as stated in the *Treatise on Awakening Mahāyāna Faith*, and that for right practice is *ning-chu pi-kuan*, or "abiding firmly in nondual meditation like a wall," as established by the first patriarch Bodhidharma, the criterion for right enlightenment, according to the Korean monk Naong of the Lin-chi tradition of *kung-an* Ch'an, is *san-kuan*, or the "three gates." This means holding the *kung-an* through unbroken inward questioning throughout the three gates of waking, dream, and deep sleep. Thus, the criterion for right enlightenment is *pu-tuan*, or "noninterruption."

My emphasis throughout has been mainly on the self-power (*jiriki*) form of faith practiced by the Ch'an tradition. However, I have also tried to interpret the other-power (*tariki*) type of faith practiced in Pure Land Buddhism. In the self-power tradition of Ch'an, faith is understood to be a kind of conviction that makes one firmly rooted in practice. In the other-power tradition of Pure Land, however, faith is understood to be a reliance on Amitābha Buddha's forty-eight primal vows to save all sentient beings. In Pure Land Buddhism, faith is the sole cause of salvation, but only because it is a gift of Amitābha's grace and universal compassion. Faith cannot be acquired by human effort but is implanted in one's heart by Amitābha when one recites his name. I have argued, however, that patriarchal faith can be expressed in an equally valid way in terms of either self-power or other-power. From the Ch'an viewpoint of self-power I can affirm that "my mind is Pure Land and my nature is Buddha," whereas from the Pure Land viewpoint of other-power I can affirm that I have *already been saved* by Amitābha's primal vows. The crucial message here is that, whether by self-power or other-power, one must arouse a patriarchal faith and not postpone one's salvation.

As I have explained at length, patriarchal faith is not a faith in the patriarchs, but the faith of the patriarchs. All Buddhist patriarchs, beings who have realized their own Buddhahood, have aroused a patriarchal faith the very moment they have attained enlightenment. One must conclude, therefore, that arousing a patriarchal faith is the key to achieving Buddhahood and becoming a patriarch oneself. Thus, in essence, I have tried to clarify the nature of the faith of the enlightened Buddhas themselves and to establish this as the criterion that all Buddhists should strive to satisfy.

In conclusion, I have tried to bridge the scholar's world and the monk's world by raising the issue of faith. In Korea, the division of Sŏn and Kyo or practice and intellectual study was the basic conflict during the Koryŏ dynasty. Chinul attempted to resolve this conflict through the issue of faith. Following Chinul and the Korean tradition of Mahāyāna Buddhism, I have emphasized faith as the key to linking Sŏn and Kyo. It can be said, borrowing the analogy of the famous Taoist sage Chuang-tzu, that faith is like a "hinge" which partakes of both Sŏn and Kyo.[3] Moreover, as a "hinge," faith participates (while yet remaining in the center) in both the unenlightened world of sentient beings and the enlightened world of Buddha. Faith is therefore truly in the Middle Way, free from all extremes. In this brief book, space would not permit an exhaustive study on the nature of faith in Mahāyāna Buddhism. However, my study will have served its purpose if it functions to open up a new field of inquiry in the area of Buddhist studies, namely, the scholarly examination of Mahāyāna Buddhism from the existential standpoint of living faith, especially what has been called throughout this book a patriarchal faith.

Abbreviations

ABORI . . . . . . Annals of' the Bhandarkar Oriental Research Institute (Poona)
AO . . . . Acta Orientalia, Copenhagen
BEFEO . . . . . . Bulletin de l'Ecole Francaise d'Extreme-Orient
EB . . . . The Eastern Buddhist, New Series
IBK . . . . Indogaku Bukkyōgaku Kenkyū
IHQ . . . . Indian Historical Quarterly
IsMEO . . . . . . Institute Italiano per il Medio e Estremo Oriente
JA . . . . Journal Asiatique, Paris
JAOS . . . . Journal of American Oriental Society, New Haven
JBORS . . . . . . Journal of the Bihar and Orissa Research Society
JBRS . . . . Journal of the Burma Research Society
JIBS . . . . Journal of Indian and Buddhist Studies (Indogaku Bukkyōgaku Kenkyū), Tokyo
JR . . . . Japanese Religions
PEW . . . . Philosophy East and West
T . . . . Taishō Shinshū Daizōkyō
Z . . . . Zokuzōkyō

Notes

Introduction

1. Since the *t'i-yung* or "essence-function" construction is originally used by East Asian Buddhists to show a non-dualistic and non-discriminate nature in their enlightenment experience, it should not exclude any other frameworks such as *neng-so* or "subject-object" construction. Nevertheless the essence-function construction must be distinguished from the subject-object construction from a scholastic perspective because the two are completely different from each other in terms of their way of thinking. For further discussions on this issue, refer to chapter 4, "Essence-Function and Subject-Object" in Part One on Faith.

2. Western scholars in the field of Hua-yen studies have little discussed the 52 stages theory of Hua-yen practice. In the traditional Hua-yen studies in the East, however, this is the main area for their discussion of faith, practice and enlightenment. The most elaborate work for this purpose is Li T'ung-hsüan's voluminous commentary entitled *Hsin hua-yen ching lun* or *Treatise on New Hua-yen Ching* (40 rolls) included in T. 1739, vol. 36, pp. 721a–1008b. See also K. Kawada's brilliant paper, entitled "Butta Kegon" or Buddha's Hua-yen included in the *Kegon shisō* or *Hua-yen Thought* (edited by H. Nakamura, Kyoto: Hōzōkan, 1960), pp. 5–79.

3. The best book on Buddhist faith published in contemporary Japan is the *Bukkyo ni okeru shin no mondai* or *Issues on Faith in Buddhism* edited by Nihon Bukkyō Gakkai or the Japanese Association for Buddhist Studies, 1963. Several papers included in the book such as Seizan Yanagida's "Kanna Zen ni okeru shin to gi no mondai" or "On Faith and Doubt in Kōan Zen" and Masao Abe's "Gendai ni okeru shin no mondai" or the "Problem of Faith in the Contemporary World" are especially excellent discussions on Zen Buddhist faith.

4. This text, sometimes referred to by its Sanskrit title, *Mahāyānaśraddhotpāda śāstra*, which was reconstructed from the Chinese title, *Ta-ch'eng ch'i-hsin lun*. although this Chinese title is usually translated into English the *Awakening of Faith in Mahāyāna*, I read it in a different way as follows: *Treatise on Awakening Mahāyāna Faith*. For its reason, refer to chapter 4, Part I in this book entitled: "Essence-Function and Subject-Object."

5. Kim, T'anhŏ, *Pojo pŏbŏ* (Seoul. Pŏppowŏn, 1963), p. 61a.

6. The basis of the Kyoto school are the monumental 19 volumes *Nishida Kitarō Zenshū* or the *Comprehensive Collection of Nishida Kitarō*, Tokyo: Iwanami shoten, 1965. For English translations of Nishida's books, see *A Study of Good* trans. by V. H. Viglielmo, 1960; *Art and Morality*, trans. by David A. Dilworth and V. Viglielmo, University of Hawaii Press, 1973; *Fundamental Problems of Philosophy*, trans. by David A. Dilworth, Sophia University, Tokyo, 1970; *Intelligibility and Philosophy of Nothingness*, trans. by R. Schinzinger, East-West Center Press, Honolulu, 1958. For an anthology of works from the Kyoto school translated into English, see *The Buddha Eye: An Anthology of the Kyoto School*, ed. Fredrick Frank, New York, Crossroad, 1982. Also, for a recent exposition on the Kyoto school written in English, see Hans Waldenfels' *Absolute Nothingness: Foundations for a Buddhist-Christian Dialogue*, tr. by J. W. Heisig, New York/Ramsey: Paulist Press, 1981.

7. For Keiji Nishitani's discussion of Great Doubt, see his *Shūkyo towa nanika* or *What is Religion?* (Tokyo: Sōbun-sha, 1961), pp. 18-26.

8. This quotation did not appear in the original Japanese version of the *Shūkyo towa nanika* or *What is Religion?* See Keiji Nishitani, "What is Religion?" included in *Philosophical Studies* 1-2, pp. 39-40.

9. For further discussions on the Great Doubt, see Chapter 9, "Questioning Meditation and the Dynamics of Faith" in Part Two on Practice.

Chapter One: The Primacy of Faith in Buddhism

1. T. 1509, vol. 25, p. 63a, lines 1-2.

2. Ibid., lines 2-4.

3. IBK III-2, p. 928.

4. This is a poem by Hsien-shou Bodhisattva found in Chapter 8, the *Ta-fang-kuang fo-hua-yen ching* or *Flower Adornment Scripture*, translated by Buddhabhadra into Chinese in A.D. 422. See T. 278, vol. 9, p. 433a, lines 26-27.

5. T. 1877, vol. 45, p. 645b, lines 22-25.

6. Ibid., p. 646a, lines 16-17.

7. T. 1666, vol. 32, p. 575b, line 16.

8. Ibid., lines 14-15.

9. For the etymological meaning of faith in Buddhism, see Matsunami Seiren's paper, "Bukkyō ni okeru shin no jii" or "The place of faith in Buddhism" included in the *Bukkyo ni okeru shin no mondai* or *Issues on Faith in Buddhism* edited by Nihon Bukkyō gakkai, Kyoto: Heirakuji shoten, 1963.

10. Augustine, *Patrologia Latina*, ed. by J. Migne, vol. 33, p. 453. Cited by James A. Mohles in his *Dimensions of Faith* (Chicago: Loyola University Press, 1969), p. 51.

11. Augustine, *Sermon 43*, Ibid., p. 46.

12. Hee Sung Keel, *Chinul: The Founder of Korean Sŏn (Zen) Tradition* (Ph.D. Thesis, Harvard University, 1977), p. 235; T'anhŏ Kim, *Pojo Pŏbŏ* (Seoul: Pŏppowŏn, 1963), p. 61b.

Chapter Two: Patriarchal Faith and Doctrinal Faith

1. T'anhŏ Kim, *Pojo pŏbŏ* (Seoul: Pŏppowŏn, 1963), pp. 61a-b.

2. T. 1739, vol. 36, p. 744b, lines 5-6; Jae-Ryong Shim, "The Philosophical Foundation of Korean Zen Buddhism: The Integration of Sŏn and Kyo by Chinul" *Journal of Social Sciences and Humanities* No. 50 (December, 1979), p. 137.

3. T. 1739, vol. 36, p. 815a, lines 4-7; Chinul, *Hwaŏmnon-chŏryo* (Chigyŏn Kim's edition, 1968), p. 2.

4. Philip B. Yampolski, *The Platform Sūtra of the Sixth Patriarch* (New York: Columbia University Press, 1967), p. 130.

5. Ibid., p. 132.

6. Hee-Jin Kim, *Dōgen Kigen-Mystical Realist* (The University of Arizona Press, 1980), p. 81.

Chapter Three: Buddha-nature and Patriarchal Faith

1. Majjhima-nikāya (Sutta 28), Vol. 1, pp. 190-1.

2. Saṃyutta-nikāya (Saṃyutta 22, 87), Vol. III, p. 120.

3. H. Ui, *Indo Tetsugaku Kenkyū*, Vol.II (Tokyo: Kōshisha shobō, 1927), pp. 261-343.

4. Nāgārjuna, *Mūlamadhyamakakārikā*. See T. 1564, p. 33b.

5. Freidrich Schleiermacher, *The Christian Faith*, ed. by H. Mackintosh and J. Steward (New York: Harper and Row Publishers, 1941), p. 68.

6. See the discussion on Tao-sheng by Kenneth Ch'en, *Buddhism in China* (Princeton University Press, 1964), pp. 112-120.

7. See Tokiwa Daijō's introductory essay on the studies of Buddha-nature in his *Busshō no kenkyū, A Study on Buddha-nature* (Tokyo, 1930), pp. 1-34.

8. Ibid., p. 25; pp. 278-308.

9. Takasaki Jikidō, *Nyoraizō shisō no keisei* (Tokyo, 1974), p. 6.

10. Ibid., p. 20; Ratnagotravibhāga I, 27.

11. Here I followed Gadjin Nagao's theory of Buddha-body in the Yogācāra tradition. See his *Chūkan to Yuishiki* (Tokyo, 1978), pp. 271-276.

12. Gadjin Nagao, "on the Theory of Buddha-Body (Buddha-kāya)" *The Eastern Buddhist*, Vol. 6, No. 1 (May 1973), pp. 36-37.

13. Ibid., p. 35 and footnote 15.

14. Ibid., p. 36 and footnote 16; See also Yoshito

Hakeda, *The Awakening of Faith* (New York, 1967), pp. 37-38.

15. The Gospel of John 14:7-11.

16. A. K. Coomaraswamy, *Buddha and the Gospel of Buddhism* (Bombay, 1956), p. 239.

Chapter Four: Essence-Function versus Subject-Object Construction

1. In the East Asian Buddhist commentary tradition, the *neng-so* construction is usually used as a syntactic device to isolate subject from object of a verb in a sentence or paragraph. However, in this book, it refers to a dualistic way of thinking in which subject and object or kāraṇa and kārya are strictly distinguished from each other.

2. T. 1985, Vol. 47, p. 500, lines 22-23; See also Seizan Yanagida's *Rinzai roku* (Tokyo: Daizō shuppan Kabushiki kaisha, 1977), pp. 139-140 and p. 258.

3. Since Professor Yung-t'ung T'ang has pointed out in his *Han Wei Liang-Chin Nan-Pei Ch'ao Fo-chiao-shih* (Shanghai, 1938, p. 333) that the concept of t'i-yung is one of the most widespread conceptual structures employed by Chinese philosophers throughout the period extending between the Wei dynasty to the Northern and Southern Dynasties, a number of papers on the subject have been published. Some of the more remarkable papers are Masatsuge Kusunomoto, "Zentai daiyō no shisō," *Nippon-chūgokugakkai-hō* (*Bulletin of the Sinological Society of Japan*) Vol. 4, 1952, pp. 76-96; Kenji Shimada, "Taiyō no rekishi ni yosete," *Tsukamoto hakushi shōju kinen bukkyō shigaku ronshū* (Kyoto, 1961), pp. 416-430; Shunei Hirai, "Chūgoku Bukkyō to taiyō shisō," *Risō* No. 549 (February, 1979), pp. 60-72.

4. Philip Yampolski, *The Platform Sūtra of the Six Patriarch* (New York, 1967), p. 137.

5. Wŏnhyo is no doubt the most celebrated personage in the history of Korean Buddhism. Wŏnhyo left an enormous legacy of philosophical treatises addressing virtually all

schools of Buddhist thought, becoming the most prolific, original, and influential writer in Korean literary history. According to Professor Myŏng-gi Cho, the author of the *Silla Pulgyo ŭi inyŏm kwa yŏksa* or *The Ideologies and History of Silla Buddhism,* Wŏnhyo wrote 98 books in about 240 rolls, of which only 20 books in 22 rolls are extant. Most of these extant books are included in a volume entitled *Han'guk pulgyo chŏnsŏ,* Vol. I (Seoul: Dongguk University Press, 1979), pp. 480–843; For articles in Japanese on Wŏnhyo, see the *Silla Wŏnhyo yŏngu* (Iri: Wŏnkwang University Press, 1979), edited by Ŭn-yong Yang.

6. The so-called three great commentaries on the *Ta-ch'eng Ch'i-hsin lun* are included in the Taisho, Vol. 44, pp. 175–287.

7. For further discussion on Wŏnhyo's t'i-yung construction, see Sung-bae Park, "A Comparative Study of Wŏnhyo and Fa-tsang on the *Ta-ch'eng ch'i-hsin lun,*" *Proceedings in the 1st International Conference on Korean Studies,* Seoul: Academy of Korean Studies, 1980.

8. T. 1844, Vol. 44, p. 203b, lines 5–7; This translation is included in the *Wŏnhyo's Commentaries on the Awakening of Faith in Mahāyāna,* Ph.D. dissertation by Sung-bae Park (University of California at Berkeley, 1979), p. 133.

9. T. 1666, Vol. 32, p. 575b, line 16.

10. See Sung-bae Park's Ph.D. dissertation, pp. 25–28.

11. D. T. Suzuki, tr. by, *Açvaghosha's Discourse on the Awakening of Faith in the Mahāyāna* (Chicago, 1900), p. 48.

12. Timothy Richard, tr. by, *The Awakening of Faith* (London: Charles Skilton, 1961), p. 39.

13. Wei Tao, tr. by, "The Awakening of Faith" *A Buddhist Bible* ed. by Dwight Goddard (Boston: Beacon Press, 1970), pp. 359–360.

14. The Editors of the Shrine of Wisdom, tr. by, *The Awakening of Faith in the Mahāyāna* (Finitry Brook, near Godalming Surrey, 1964), p. 23.

15. Yoshito Hakeda, *The Awakening of Faith* (New York, 1967), pp. 23–24.

16. Richard Robinson, tr. by, *Treatise on the Awakening*

of Faith in Mahāyāna (unpublished mimeographed edition), p. 3.

17. Yoshito Hakeda, *The Awakening of Faith* (New York, 1967), p. 28.

Chapter Five: Nonbacksliding Faith and Backsliding Faith

1. T. 1666, Vol. 32, p. 580b, lines 25-26' Yoshito Hakeda, *The Awakening of Faith* (New York, 1967), p. 81.

2. Van A. Harvey, *A Handbook of Theological Terms* (New York: Macmillan Publishing Co., 1974), pp. 95-98.

3. Daiei Kaneko, "Shinarn no tariki shinjin," *Bukkyō no Konpon shinri* edited by Shōson Miyamoto (Tokyo: Sanseido, 1957), pp. 1093-1112.

4. T. 1666, vol. 32, p. 580b, lines 18-580c, line 5; Yoshito Hakeda, *The Awakening of Faith* (New York, 1967), pp. 80-82.

5. The Old Testament, Genesis 22:1-14.

Chapter Six: The Two Truths and Skill-in-Means

1. Yoshio Nishi, "Shinzoku nitaisetsu no kōzō," *Bukkyō no konpon shinri* (Tokyo, 1957), pp. 197-218.

2. Ibid., p. 197; See Kenneth K. Inada's *Nāgārjuna: A Translation of his Mūlamadhyamakakārikā with an Introductory Essay* (Tokyo: Hokuseido Press, 1970), p. 146, verses 8, 9, and 10.

3. T. 262, Vol 9, p. 12b-c; See Leon Hurvitz, *Scripture of the Lotus Blossom of the Fine Dharma* (Columbia University Press, 1976), pp. 59-64.

4. Sŏng-chŏl Lee, *Winter Retreat Sermons* (unpublished mimeographed edition, Haeinsa Korea, 1967), p. 16.

Chapter Seven: The Unity of Faith and Enlightenment in Practice

1. Hee-Jin Kim, *Dōgen Kigen—Mystical Realist* (The University of Arizona Press, 1980), p. 79.

2. Ibid., p. 68.

3. Philip Yampolski, *The Platform sutra of the sixth Patriarch* (Columbia University Press, 1967), p. 135.

4. Ibid., p. 137.

Chapter Eight: Bodhidharma's Wall Meditation

1. Hakuju Ui, *Zenshūshi kenkyū* (Tokyo: Iwanami shoten, 1939), pp. 1-90.

2. Seizan Yanagida, *Zen shisō* (Tokyo: Chūkō shinsho 400, 1975), p. 23.

3. Kyŏnghŏ ed. by, *Sŏnmun Ch'waryo* (Pusan: Pŏmŏsa, 1968), p. 137; D. T. Suzuki, *Manual of Zen Buddhism* (New York: Grove Press, 1978), pp. 73-74; Seizan Yanagida, *Zen shisō*, p. 15.

4. It is notable that this text also emphasizes the primacy of faith as we do and does not devaluate the importance of scriptures as later Ch'an masters do.

5. We can see in the text some influences from the *Vajra-samādhi sūtra* or the *Diamond Meditation Sūtra* (Chin-kang san-mei ching, T. 273, Vol. 9, pp. 365-374b). See Hakuju Ui, *Zenshūshi Kenkyū* (Iwanami shoten, 1939), pp. 23-24.

6. Seizan Yanagida, *Zen shisō* (Chūkō shinsho, 1975), p. 22.

Chapter Nine: Questioning Meditation and the Dynamics of Faith

1. There is no reliable book on *Kōan* meditation in either the East or the West. Although the *Pi-yen lu* or the *Blue Cliff Record* (tr. by Thomas and J. C. Cleary, Shambhala, 1977) is known as the best book for understanding Kōan Zen in East Asia, the famous Ch'an master Ta-hui (1089-1163), the direct and beloved disciple of Yüan-wu (1063-1135), the main author of the book, burned it up. However, in the West, several books on Kōan are popular: Ruth Fuller Sasaki et al, *The Zen Kōan* (A Harvest Book, 1965); Yoel Hoffmann, *The Sound of the One Hand* (New York: Basic Books, 1975).

2. Shōkin Furuta, "Kōan no rekishiteki hatten keitai ni

okeru shinrisei no mondai" included in Shōson Miyamoto, ed. *Bukkyō no konpon shinri*, Tokyo: Sanseidō, 1957).

3. Kao-feng, *Ch'an-yao* (edited by Chin-ho An, Seoul: Mansanghoe, 1956), pp. 26a–b.

4. Philip Kapleau, *The Three Pillars of Zen* (New York: Anchor Books, 1980), pp. 64–66.

5. Sören Kierkegaard, "Concluding Unscientific Postcript" in *Classical Statements of Faith and Reason*, ed. L. Miller (New York: Random House, 1970), p. 165.

6. Ibid., p. 167.

7. Ibid., pp. 153–154.

8. Ibid., p. 158.

9. Ibid., p. 158.

10. Paul Tillich, *Dynamics of Faith* (Harper Colophon Books, 1957), p. 20.

11. Ibid., p. 22.

12. Ibid., p. 99, p. 102.

13. Ibid., p. 17.

14. Wu-men, *Wu-men Kuan*, T. 2005, Vol. 48, pp. 292–299. See Zenkei Shibayama, *Zen Comments on the Mumonkan* (Mentor, 1974), p. 32.

15. Keiji Nishitani, *Shūkyo towa nanika*, (Tokyo: Sōbun-sha, 1961), pp. 18–26.

16. T. 2005, Vol. 48, p. 292.

17. Shibayama, op.cit., p. 19–20.

18. Ibid., p. 24.

19. T. 2005, Vol. 48, p. 293a, lines 13–14.

Chapter Ten: Practice in the *Treatise on Awakening Mahāyāna Faith*

1.For Wŏnhyo's *Haedongso*, see Sung-bae Park's dissertation, *Wŏnhyo's commentaries on the Treatise on Awakening of Faith in Mahāyāna* (University of California at Berkeley, 1979), pp. 120–185. This quotation appears on p. 148.

2. Ibid., p. 149.

3. See Yoshito Hakeda's explanation on the four marks, in his *The Awakening of Faith*, p. 39.

4. T. 1666, Vol. 32, p. 576b, lines 18-28.

5. Ibid., p. 576a, lines 5-7; see also Y. Hakeda's *The Awakening of Faith*, p. 31.

6. T. 1844, Vol. 44, p. 203z, lines 20-38.

7. Ibid., p. 204b, lines 6-10.

8. T. 1666, Vol. 32, p. 581c.

9. T. 1844, Vol. 44, p. 204b, lines 24-27.

Chapter Eleven: Faith and Practice in Pure Land Buddhism

1. Yoshito Hakeda, *The Awakening of Faith*, (Columbia University Press, 1967), p. 102.

2. See Sung-bae Park's dissertation, Wŏnhyo's commentaries on the *Awakening of Faith in Mahāyāna* (University of California at Berkeley, 1979), pp. 45-57.

3. Daiei Kaneko, *Kyōgyōshinshō*, Tokyo: Iwanami Bunko, 1958.

4. The *Amitābha Sūtra. See T. 367, Vol. 12, p. 348a.*

5. Alfred Bloom, *Shinran's Gospel of Pure Grace* (The University of Arizona Press, 1981), pp. 61-62.

Chapter Twelve: Faith as the Practice of Compassion

1. Schubert M. Ogden, *Faith and Freedom* (Nashville: Abingdon, 1979), p. 64.

2. Nāgārjuna, the *Mahāprajñāpāramitā-śāstra* or the *Ta-chih-tu lun*. See T. 1509, Vol. 25, p. 350b, lines 25-28.

3. Wŏnhyo, the *Haedongso*. See Sung-bae Park's dissertation, pp. 138-139.

4. The Gospel of Matthew 5:43-48.

5. Keiji Nishitani, *Shūkyo towa nanika* (Tokyo: Sōbunsha, 1961), pp. 66-70.

Chapter Thirteen: Sudden Enlightenment and Gradual Practice

1. Sung-bae Park, "Korean Monk Chinul's Theory of Sudden Enlightenment and Gradual Practice," *Asian Culture*, Vol. VIII, No. 4, 1980.

2. Tsung-mi, *Fa-chi pieh-hsing lu* included in Chinul's *Pŏpchip Pyŏrhaengnok Chŏryo* ed. by Chinho An, Seoul, 1957.

3. Tsung-mi, *A Commentary on the Yüan-chiao ching*. See T. 1795, Vol. 39, p. 552c, lines 23-25.

4. See Chung-feng, *Shan-fang yeh-hua* included in *Chung-feng kuang-lu* (Pulguksa, 1977), p. 58a-b; Hung Chiao-fan, *Lin-chieh lu* (Z. 1-2b-21, 4), pp. 296-297.

Chapter Fourteen: Faith and Enlightenment in the *Hua-yen Sūtra*

1. Yukio Sakamato, "Hokkai yengi no rekishiteki keisei," *Bukkyō no Konpon Shinri* (Ed. by Shōson Miyamoto, Sanseido, 1957), pp. 891-932.

2. Francis H. Cook, *Hua-yen Buddhism: The Jewel Net of India* (The Pennsylvania State University Press, 1977), pp. 1-19.

3. T. 1870, Vol. 45, p. 580c, lines 5-8.

4. T'anhŏ Kim, *Hwaŏmgyŏng ch'onggang* (unpublished mimeographed edition, Odaesan, 1977, appendix 1.

5. Chinul, *Wŏndon sŏngbullon*, included in T'anhŏ Kim's *Pojo pŏbŏ* (Seoul, 1963), pp. 91-120.

6. T'anhŏ Kim, *Hwaŏmgyŏng ch'onggang* (Odaesan, 1977), pp. 8-10.

7. T. 1739, Vol. 36, p. 818b, lines 7-14.

8. Ibid., p. 818b, lines 14-19.

9. D. T. Suzuki, *Studies in the Lankāvatara sutra* (London, 1930), pp. 230-236.

10. Hua-yen scholars in Korea such as Chinul and T'anho Kim discuss this problem seriously throughout all their writings. See especially, T'anho Kim's *Shin Hwaŏmgyŏng hamnon*, Seoul: Hwaŏmhak yŏnguso, 1977.

11. T'anhŏ Kim, *Hwaŏmgyŏng ch'onggang* (Odaesan, 1977), appendix 2.

12. Chinul, *Hwaŏmnon chŏryo* (Chigyŏn Kim's edition, Tokyo, 1968), p. 451.

13. T. 2010, Vol. 48, pp. 376b-377a; D. T. Suzuki, *Manual of Zen Buddhism* (Grove Press, 1978), pp. 81-82.

Chapter Fifteen: *Kkaech'im:* The Experience of Brokenness

1. Sung-bae Park, "On Wŏnhyo's Enlightenment," *IBK* (Vol. XX19, No. 1, December 1980), pp. 467-470.
2. See Chinul's *Kanhwa kyŏrŭilon* (T'anhŏ Kim's edition, Seoul, 1963), pp. 121-138.
3. T. 2005, Vol. 48, p. 293a, line 13.

Chapter Sixteen: Revolution of the Basis

1. T. 1844, Vol. 44, p. 203b, lines 17-19.
2. D. T. Suzuki, *Studies in the Lankāvatara Sūtra* (London, 1930), pp. 182-199.
3. For further discussion on Yogācāra doctrine of change, see Gadjin Nagao's *Chūkan to Yuishiki* (Iwanami shoten, 1978), pp. 239-244.
4. Ibid., pp. 279-280; Gadjin Nagao, "On the Theory of Buddha-Body," *The Eastern Buddhist*, Vol. VI, No. 1 (May 1973), p. 44.

Chapter Seventeen: The Three Gates

1. Sŏng-chŏl Lee, *Winter Sermons* (unpublished memeographed edition, Haeinsa, 1967), pp. 18-20.
2. Ibid., p. 32.
3. Ibid., p. 136.
*4. Ibid., p. 124.

Conclusion

1. Later Ch'an masters emphasis on the nonbacksliding from the patriarchal faith is comparable to Early Mahāyānists' emphasis on nonbacksliding from Mahāyāna faith.
2. Here patriarchal faith means nothing but Buddha's faith in which there is no distinction at all between the Buddha and sentient beings. Thus Buddhas have universal compassion for all sentient beings.
3. Burton Watson, tr. by, *The Complete Works of Chuang Tzu* (Columbia University Press, 1968), pp. 29-49.

A Glossary of Chinese Characters

*[Japanese and Korean words are signified by the
letters (J) and (K) respectively.]*

Abe Masao (J)　阿部正雄

Amida (J)　阿弥陀

Amidakyō (J)　阿弥陀経

An Chin-ho (K)　安震湖

Bukkyō ni okeru shin no mondai (J)　仏教における信の問題

Bukkyō ni okeru shin no chii (J)　仏教における信の地位

Busshō no kenkyū (J)　仏性の研究

Ch'an　禪

Ch'an-yao　禪要

Chao-chou　趙州

Cheng-hsin　正信

chen-ju　眞如

Chen-ju hsiang　眞如相

Ch'eng-kuan　澄觀

Cheng-ting Chü　正定聚

Chiao-hsin　教信

Chieh-hsin　解信

Chien-sheng　見性

Ch'i-hsin　起信

Chih-kuan　止觀

Chih-yen　智儼

Chi-gyon Kim (K)　金知見

Ching-hsin　淨信

Chin-kang san-mei ching　金剛三昧經

Chinul (K)　知訥

Chogye (K) 曹溪

Chosil Sunim (K) 祖室스님

Cho-shin (K) 祖信

Chuang Tzu 莊子

Chūgoku Bukkyō to taiyō shisō (J) 中國仏教と体用思想

Chūkan to yuishiki (J) 中観と唯識

Chūkō shinsho (J) 中公新書

Chung-feng 中峯

Chung-feng kuang-lu 中峯廣錄

dai-funshi (J) 大憤志

daigi (J) 大疑

daigidan (J) 大疑団

dai-shinkon (J) 大信根

Daizō shuppan kabushiki kaisha (J) 大藏出版株式会社

Dōgen (J) 道元

Dōgen Kigen (J) 道元希玄

Dongguk (K) 東國

D. T. Suzuki (J) 鈴木大拙

Fa-hsiang 法相

fa-hsin 發心

Fa-tsang 法藏

Furuta Shōkin (J) 古田紹欽

Gendai ni okeru shin no mondai (J) 現代における信の問題

Gyōnen (J) 凝然

Haedongso (K) 海東疏

Hokkai engi no rekishiteki keisei (J) 法界緣起の歷史的形成

Han'guk pulgyo chŏnsŏ (K) 韓國佛教全書

Han Wei Liang-Chin Nan-Pei Ch'ao Fo-Chiao-Shih 漢魏兩晋南北朝佛教史

Haeinsa (K) 海印寺

Heirakuji shoten (J) 平樂寺書店

Hirai Shunei (J)　平井俊榮

Hokuseidō (J)　北星堂

Hōzōkan (J)　法藏館

hsiang　相

Hsien-shou　賢首

hsin　信，心

hsin-hsin　信心

Hsin-hsin ming　信心銘

Hsin Hua-yen-ching lun　新華嚴經論

hsing-ch'i　性起

hsing-ju　行入

Hsüan-hua　宣化

Hsüan-tsang　玄奘

Hua-yen　華嚴

Hua-yen ching　華嚴經

hua t'ou shun shu　話頭純熟

hu-fa　護法

hui　慧

Hui-hsiang　迴向

Hui-neng　惠能

Hui-yüan　慧遠

Hung Chiao-fan　洪覺範

Hu Shih　胡適

hwadu (K)　話頭

hwajaeng (K)　和諍

Hwaŏmgyŏng ch'onggang (K)　華嚴經總講

Hwaŏmhak yŏnguso (K)　華嚴學研究所

Hwaŏmnon chŏryo (K)　華嚴論節要

i-hsin　一心

Ikan (J)　惟寬

[161]

Indogaku bukkyōgaku kenkyū (J) 印度学仏教学研究

Indo tetsugaku kenkyū (J) 印度哲学研究

Iri (K) 裡里

it'uan tulu 疑團獨露

Iwanami bunko (J) 岩波文庫

Iwanami shoten (J) 岩波書店

Jae-Ryong Shim (K) 沈在龍

jiriki (J) 自力

ju-lai hsing-ch'i 如來性起

kabe ga miru (J) 壁が見る

kanhwa (K) 看話

Kanhwa Kyŏrŭiron (K) 看話決疑論

Kaneko Daiei (J) 金子大榮

Kanna zen ni okeru shin to gi no mondai (J) 看話禪における 信と疑の問題

Kao-feng 高峰

kap'i (K) 加被

Kawada (J) 川田

Kegon shisō (J) 華嚴思想

kenshō (J) 見性

Kim T'anhŏ (K) 金吞虛

Kishillonso (K) 起信論疏

kkaech'ida (K) 깨치다

kkaeda (K) 깨다

kkaech'im (K) 깨침

kkaejida (K) 깨지다

Kōan (J) 公案

Kōan no rekishiteki hatten keitai ni okeru shinrisei no mondai (J) 公案の歴史的發展型態にむける眞理性の問題

Kōan Zen (J) 公案禪

Kong'an (K) 公案

Kong'an Sŏn (K) 公案禪

Koryŏ (K) 高麗

Kuang-ming chaio 光明覺

K'uei-chi 窺基

kung-an 公案

Kusunomoto Masatsuge (J) 楠本正継

Kyo (K) 教

Kyōgyōshishō (J) 教行信證

Kyŏnghŏ (K) 鏡虛

Kyŏngsang (K) 慶尚

Kyoshin (K) 教信

Kyoto (J) 京都

li-ju 理入

Lin-chi 臨濟

Lin-chieh lu 林間錄

li-nien 離念

li-shih wu-ai 理事無礙

Li T'ung-hsüan 李通玄

Matsunami Seiren (J) 松濤誠廉

Miao-chiao 妙覺

Miyamoto shōson (J) 宮本正尊

mu (K, J) 無

Myung-gi Cho (K) 趙明基

Nagao Gadjin (J) 長尾雅人

Nakamura (J) 中村

neng-so 能所

nien-fo 念佛

Nihon bukkyō gakkai (J) 日本仏教学会

ning-chu 凝住

ning-chu kuan 凝住觀

ning-chu pi-kuan 凝住壁觀

Nippon Chūgokugakkai-hō (J) 日本中國學會報

Nishida Kitarō (J) 西田幾多郎

Nishida Kitarō zenshū (J) 西田幾多郎全集

Nishitani Keiji (J) 西谷啓治

Nishi Yoshio (J) 西義雄

Nyoraizō shisō no keisei (J) 如來藏思想の形成

Odaesan (K) 五台山

pen-chiao 本覺

pi 壁

pi-kuan 壁觀

Pi-yen lu 碧巖錄

Pojo pŏbŏ (K) 普照法語

Pŏmŏsa (K) 梵魚寺

Pŏpchip pyŏrhaengnok chŏryo (K) 法集別行錄節要

Pŏppowŏn (K) 法寶院

pu-chiao 不覺

pu-erh 不二

Pulguksa (K) 佛國寺

Pusan (K) 釜山

pu-sui wen-chiao 不隨文教

pu-tuan 不斷

pu-t'ui 不退

pu-t'ui hsin 不退信

Rinzai (J) 臨濟

Rinzai roku (J) 臨濟錄

Saigusa (J) 三枝

Sakamoto Yukio (J) 坂本幸男

sam-kwan (K) 三關

san-kuan　三關

Sanseidō (J)　三省堂

Sekiguchi (J)　關口

Seng-t'san　僧璨

Shan-fang yeh-hua　山房夜話

Shao-lin　少林

She-lun　攝論

Shen-hsiu　神秀

sheng-mieh　生滅

sheng-mieh hsiang　生滅相

she-wang kuei-chen　捨妄歸眞

shih-chu　十住

shih-hsin　十信

shih-shih wu-ai　事事無礙

Shimada Kenji (J)　島田虔次

shin (K, J)　信

Shinran (J)　親鸞

Shinran no tariki shinshin (J)　親鸞の他力信心

Shin Hwaŏmgyŏng hamnon (K)　新華嚴經合論

Shinzoku nitaisetsu no kōzō (J)　眞俗二諦說の構造

Shōbōgenzō (J)　正法眼藏

shōjō no shu (J)　證上の修

shōzen no shu (J)　證前の修

Shūkyō towa nanika (J)　宗教とは何か

Shushō-ichinyo (J)　修證一如

Silla pulgyo ŭi inyŏm kwa yŏksa (K)　新羅佛教의理念과歷史

Silla Wŏnhyo yŏngu (K)　新羅元曉研究

Sōbunsha (J)　創文社

sŏn (K)　禪

Sŏnmun Ch'waryo (K)　禪門撮要

Sōtō (J) 曹洞

Sung-bae Park (K) 朴 性焙

Sung-chŏl Lee (K) 李性徹

sunim (K) 스님

ta-ch'eng 大乘

Ta-ch'eng ch'i-hsin lun 大乘起信論

Ta-ch'eng i-chang 大乘義章

Ta-chih-tu lun 大智度論

Ta-fang-kuang fo-hua-yen ching 大方廣佛華嚴經

Ta-hui 大慧

Taishō (J) 大正

Taishō shinshū daizōkyo (J) 大正新修大藏經

ta-i 大疑

Taiyō no rekishi ni yosete (J) 体用の歴史に寄せて

Takasaki Jikido (J) 高崎直道

Takeuchi Yoshinori (J) 武内義雄

Takusui (J) 澤水

T'ang Yung-t'ung 湯用彤

ta-pei 大悲

Ta-p'in nieh-pan-ching 大品涅槃經

tao 道

Tao-sheng 道生

tariki (J) 他力

t'i-hsiang-yung 體相用

ting 定

ti-pa mo-chieh 第八魔界

t'i-yung 体用

Tokiwa Daijō (J) 常盤大定

t'ong pulgyo (K) 通佛教

tono-chŏmsu (K) 頓悟漸修

[166]

tsu-hsin　祖信

Tsukamoto hakushi shōju kinen bukkyō shigaku ronshū (J)
塚本博士頌壽記念仏教史學論集

Tsung-mi　宗密

t'ui-hsin　退信

tun-wu tun-hsiu　頓悟頓修

Ui Hakuju (J)　宇井伯壽

Ŭn-yong Yang (K)　梁銀容

wen-hsin　聞信

Wŏnhyo (K)　元曉

Wŏnkwang (K)　圓光

wu　無

wu-ai　無礙

Wu-men　無門

Wu-men kuan　無門關

wu-sheng fa-jen　無生法忍

Yanagida Seizan (J)　柳田聖山

Yen-Shou　延壽

Yüan-chiao ching　圓覺經

yüan-ch'i　緣起

Yüan-wu　圓悟

yu fa neng-c'hi mo-ho-yen hsin-ken
有法能起摩訶衍信根

Yung-ming　永明

yung-t'ung　融通

Zen (J)　禪

Zen shisō (J)　禪思想

Zenshūshi kenkyū (J)　禪宗史研究

Zentai daiyō no shisō (J)　全體大用の思想

Zokuzōkyō (J)　續藏經

Bibliography

I. Chinese Sources

Chen-ti (Paramārtha), tr. by, *Ta-ch'eng ch'i-hsin lun.* T. 1666, vol. 32, pp. 575a–583b.

Fa-tsang. *Ta-ch'eng ch'i-hsin lun i-chi.* T. 1846, vol. 44, pp. 240c–287b.

———. *Ta-ch'eng ch'i-hsin lun i-chi pieh-chi.* T. 1847, vol. 44, pp. 287b–295c.

Fung Yu-lan. *Chung-kuo che-hsüeh shih.* Hong Kong, 1975.

Hui-yüan. *Ta-ch'eng ch'i-hsin lun i-su.* T. 1843, vol. 44, pp. 175a–201c.

———. *Ta-ch'eng i chang.* T. 1851, vol. 44, pp. 465–875c.

Hu Shih, ed. by, *Shen-hui ho-shang i-chi.* Taipei: Hu Shih chi-nien kuan, 1971.

———. *Hu Shih ch'an-hsüeh an.* Taipei: Cheng Chung shu-chü, 1975.

Li T'ung-hsüan. *Hsin hua-yen-ching lun.* T. 1739, vol. 36, pp. 721a–1008b.

Śīkshānanda, tr. by, *Ta-fang-kuang fo-hua-yen ching.* T. 279, vol. 10, pp. 1–444.

T'ang Chün-i. *Chung-kuo che-hsüeh yüan-lun.* Hongkong, 1966.

T'ang Yung-t'ung. *Han Wei Liang-Chin Nan-pei-ch'ao fo-chiao shih.* Taipei: T'ing-wen shu-chü, 1975.

II. Korean Sources

Chinul. *Hwaŏmnon chŏryo*, ed. by Kim Chigyŏn. Tokyo: Seifū Gakuen, 1968.

Chinul. *Pŏpchip pyŏrhaengnok chŏryo pyŏng'ip sagi.* Contained in Sajip happon, ed. by An Chin-ho. Seoul, 1957.

Cho Myŏng-gi. *Silla pulgyo ŭi inyŏm kwa yŏksa.* Seoul: Shin t'aeyangsa, 1962.

Choe Min Hong. *Han'guk ch'ŏrhak*. Seoul: Sŏngmunsa, 1969.

Choe Namsŏn. "Chosŏn pulgyo," *Pulgyo*. 1930, 74:n.i.

————, "Pak munhwaron," *Shindong-A*. Seoul, 1972.

Ha Tae-Hŭng and Mintz, Grafton K., tr. by, *Samguk yusa*. Seoul: Yŏnsei University Press, 1972.

Han Ki-du. *Han'guk pulgyo sasang*. Iri, Chŏlla Pukto, 1973.

————. *Silla sidae ŭi sŏn sasang*. Iri, 1974.

————. "Han'guk ŭi sŏnji," *Han'guk pulgyo sasang*. Iri, Chŏlla Pukto, 1973.

Hyŏn Sang Yun. *Chosŏn sasangsa*. Seoul, 1949.

Iryŏn. *Samguk yusa*. T. 2039, vol. 49, pp. 953-1019.

Kim T'anhŏ, tr. by. *Pojo pŏbŏ*. Seoul: Pŏppowŏn, 1963.

————, ed. and tr. by, *Shin hwaŏmgyŏng hamnon*. 23 vols. Seoul: Hwaŏmhak yŏnguso, 1977.

Kim Yŏngsu. "Chogye Sŏnjong e ch'wihaya," *Chindan hakpo*. No. 9 (1938), pp. 145-175.

————, "Chosŏn pulgyo chongji e ch'wihaya," *Pulgyo sin*, No. 8-9 (1937-1938).

Kim Yŏng-t'ae et al. *Han'guk pulgyosa*. Seoul: Chinsudang, 1970.

Ko Ikchin. "Wŏnhyo ŭi kishillonso pyŏlgi rŭl t'ong'hae pon chinsok-wŏlyung-muaegwan kwa kŭ sŏng'ip iron;" *Pulgyo hakpo*. Vol. 10. Seoul: Dongguk University, 1937, pp. 287-321.

————. "Wŏnhyo sasung ŭi silch'ŏn wŏlli," *Han'guk pulgyo sasangsa*, pp. 225-255, Sungsan Pak Kiljin paksa hwagap kinyŏm saŏphoe: Iri, Korea, 1975.

Koryŏ taejanggyŏng. Photo-reprint, Seoul: Dongguk University, 1976.

Kyŏnghŏ, ed. by, *Sŏnmun ch'waryo*. Pusan: Pŏmŏ Monastery, 1968.

Lee Chong-ik. *Wŏnhyo ŭi kŭnbon sasang*. Seoul: Tongbang sasang yŏn'guwŏn, 1977.

Lee Ŭl Ho. "Han sasang ŭi kujojŏk sŏngkyŏk kwa yŏksajŏk mengnak," *Kŭmhyang munhwa*, Vol. 1. Kwangjoo: Kŭmhyang Jaedan, 1981.

Lew Seung Kook. "Han'guk yuhak sasang sŏsŏl," *Han'guk minjok sasang daegye*. Seoul: Korea University Press, 1970.

Park Chong-hong. *Han'guk sasangsa*. Seoul: Sŏmundang, 1972.

Park Sung Bae. "Moguja ŭi o wa su e taehayŏ," *Han'guk sasang chongsŏ II*, Seoul: Kyŏng in munhwasa, 1975, pp. 79-100.

————. "Moguja ŭi saeng'ae wa sasang tŭkching," *Simwon*, 1964, 1:1, pp. 27-41.

————. "O ŭi munje," *Dongguk sasang*, 1963, 2: pp. 23-36.

————. "Pojo : chŏnghye ssangsu ŭi kuhyŏnja," *Han'guk ŭi in'gansang*, Vol. III: *Chonggyoga, sahoe pongsaja p'yŏn*, Seoul, 1965, pp. 143-154.

————. "Wŏnhyo sasang chŏn'gae ŭi munjejŏm," *Tongsŏ ch'ŏrhak ŭi chemunje*, festschrift for Dr. Kyu-young Kim, Seoul 1979.

Rhi Ki-Young. "Han'guk pulgyo ŭi kŭnbon sasang kwa saeroun ŭimi," *Han'guk minjok munhwasa*. Seoul: Han'guk jŏngshin munhwawŏn, 1978.

————, tr. by *Han'guk ŭi pulgyo sasang*. Seoul: Samsŏng ch'ulp'ansa, 1978.

————. *Wŏnhyo sasang*. Seoul: Hongbŏpwŏn, 1967.

Sŏsan. *Sŏn'ga kwigam*. Z. 2, 17, V.

————. *Sŏn'gyo sŏk*, Contained in the *Ch'ŏng'hŏd'ang chip*, roll 4, pp. 37-43.

Wŏnhyo. *Taesŭng kishllon pyŏlgi*. 2 rolls, T. 1845, Vol. 44, pp. 226a-240c.

————. *Taesŭng kishillonso*. 2 rolls, T. 1844, vol. 44, pp. 202a-226a.

Yi Hŭi-su. *T'och'akhwa kwajŏng esŏ pon Han'guk pulgyo*. Seoul, 1971.

Yi Nŭng-hwa. *Chosŏn pulgyo t'ongsa*. Seoul: Sinmungwan, 1918.

Yu Dong-Shik. *Minsok chonggyo wa Han'guk munhwa*. Hyŏndae sasang ch'ongsŏ 27. Seoul: Hyŏndae sasangsa, 1978.

Yun Sŏng-Bŏm. *The Korean Theology*. Seoul: Sungmyŏng munhwasa, 1972.

III. Japanese Sources

Akanuma Chizen. "Kishin ron no shinnyo ni tsuite," *Ōtani gakuhō*, 1, 1929.

Andō Toshio. *Tendai shōgu shisōron*. Kyoto: Hōzōkan, 1973.

Araki Kengo. *Bukkyō to jukyō*. Kyoto: Heirakuji, 1963.

————. tr. by, *Zen no goroku* (17): *Daie-sho*. Tokyo, 1969.

Bukkyo ni okeru shin no mondai. Ed. by Nihon bukkyo gakkai. Kyoto: Heirakuji shoten, 1963.

Eda Shunyū. "Chōsen zen no keisei—'Fushōzen' no seikaku ni tsuite," *Indogaku bukkyōgaku kenkyū*, V, No. 2 (1957), pp. 351-359.

Furuta Shōkin. "Keihō Shūmitsu no kenkyū," *Shina bukkyō shigaku*, vol. 2, no. 2, 1938, pp. 83-97.

Fuse Kōgaku. *Nehanshū no kenkyū*, 2 vols., Tokyo: Kokusho kankōkai, 1973.

Hattori masa'aki. "Busshōron no ichi kōsatsu," *Bukkyō shigaku*, IV, No. 3 and 4, 1955.

Higure Kyōyū. "Kishin ron ni okeru butsu sanjin no gengo o ronzu," *Shūkyō Kenkyū*, 6-3, 1929.

Hirai Shun'ei. "Sanron gakuha no genryū keifu—Kashō ni okeru kanga kyūsetsu o megutte," *Tōhōgaku*, No. 28, 1964, pp. 52-65.

Hirakawa Akira. *Daijō Kishinron*. Tokyo: Daizō shuppan, 1973.

Hirose Bungō. "Kishin ron ni okeru ninshiki jissen no sansō," *Tetsugaku kenkyū*, 15-171, 1930.

Hisamatsu Shin'ichi. "Kishin no kadai," *Tetsugaku kenkyū*, Nos. 354 and 355, 1946.

Ikeda Rosan. "Tendaigaku kara enton no kannen ni tsuite," IBK vol. 22, 1973, pp 307-310.

Imazu Kōgaku. *Daijō kishin ron* in *Bukkyō daikei*. Tokyo: Bukkyō daikei kankōkai, 1918.

Ishibashi Shinkai. "Gangyo no kegon shisō," JIBS. XIX, No. 2, 1971.

Ishii Kyōdō. *Kegonkyōgaku seiritsu shi.* Kyoto, 1956.

Itō Giken. "Daijō kishin ron no kentō," *Daijo*, 22:7-12, 1943.

Itō Kazuo. *"Kishin ron ni okeru shinnyo no rikai," Nippon bukkyō gakkai nempo*, vol. 14, 1942.

Kamada Shigeo. *Chūgoku bukkyō shi kenkyū.* Shunjūsha, 1968.

————. Chūgoku kegon shisōshi no kenkyū. Tokyo: Tōkyō daigaku, 1965.

————. "Chūgoku zen shisō keisei no kyōgakuteki haikei — daijō kishin ron o chūshin toshite," *Tōyō bunka kenkyūsho kiyō*, vol. 49, 1969.

————. Shūmitsu kyōgaku no shisōshi teki kenkyū. Tokyo: Tōkyō daigaku, 1975.

————. tr. by, *Zengen shosenshū tojo (Zen no goroku vol. 9).* Tokyo: Chikuma shobō, 1971.

Kashiwagi Hiroo. "Nyoraizō no engi shisō," *Tōyō shisō.* Tokyo, 1967.

————. "Kishin ron ni okeru shinjōju hosshin ni tsuite," Indogaku bukkyōgaku kenkyū, 16:2, 1968.

Katsumata Shunkyō. *Bukkyō ni okeru shinshikisetsu no kenkyū.* Tokyo, 1961

Kawada Kumatarō and Nakamura Hajime, ed. by, *Kegon shisō.* Kyoto: Hōzōkan, 1960.

Kimura Kiyotaka. *Shoki chūgoku kegon shisō no kenkyū.* Tokyo: Shunjūsha, 1977.

Kitamura Kyōgon. "Kishin ron no kunshu setsu," Shūkyō zasshi, 9:3,5, 1905.

Kobayashi Jitsugen. "Kishinron kaishaku no hensen: kegon kyōgaku tenkai no kontei to shite," *Indogaku bukkyōgaku kenkyū*, vol. 13, 2, 1965, pp. 668-671.

————. "Kishin ron ni okeru nyoraizō no kaku, fukaku no mondai," *Indogaku bukkyōgaku kenkyū*, 12:2, 1964.

Kōno Hōun. "Kishin ron no ariyashiki ni tsuite," *Mujintō*, 22:7, 1917.

————. "Kishin ron no shoshū ni oyobosu eikyō," *Rokujō gakuhō*, 89, 90, 92, 96, 1909.

————. "Kishin ron shosetsu no ariyashiki to yuishikiron," *Ōsaki gakuhō*, 23, 1970.

————. "Kishin ron to yuishiki ron to no sōi," *Misshū gakuhō*, 12, 1914.

Kōno Shigeo. "Daijō kishin ron ni okeru shujōshin ni tsuite," *Indogaku bukkyōgaku kenkyū*, 21:2, 1973.

Kubota Ryōen. *Shina ju dō butsu kōshōshi*. Tokyo: Daitō shuppansha, 1943.

————. *Shina ju dō butsu sangyō shiron*. Tokyo, 1931.

Maeda Eun. "Kishin ron no ganki jōdo no dan to iko hon tono hikaku," *Rokujo gakuhō*, 100, 1910.

Matsubayashi Hiroyuki. "Shiragi Jōdokyō no ichi kōsatsu — Gangyō no Jōdokyō shisō o megutte." IBK XV-I, 1966.

Matsunami Seiren. *Bukkyō ni okeru shin to gyō*. Heirakuji shoten, 1967.

————. "Kishin ron no kan ni tsuite," *Bukkyō ronso*, 6, 1958.

————. "Kishin ron—shisō no taikei to nendai," *Nihon bukkyō gakkai nempō*, No. 22, March 1956, pp. 143-160.

Michibata Ryōshū. *Chūgoku Bukkyō shi*. Kyoto, 1965.

Mishina Shōei. "Chosen ni okeru Bukkyō to minzoku shinkō," *Bukkyō shigaku*, No. 4, 1954, pp. 9-32.

————. "Shiragi no Jōdokyō—'Sankoku iji' shosai Jōdokyō kankei kiji chūkai," *Tsukamoto Hakase shōju kinen bukkyō shigaku ronshū*, Kyoto, 1961, pp. 727-745.

Miyamoto Shōson. *Bukkyo no konpon shinri* Tokyo: San-seidō, 1974.

————. *Chūdo shisō oyobi sono hattatsu*. Kyōto: Hōzōkan, 1944.

————. "Konpon fumbetsu no kenkyū," *MT*, pp. 353-498.

Mochizuki Shinkō. "Kishin ron to sensatsukyō tono ruidō oyobi kankei," *Bukkyō gaku zasshi*, 1:5, 1920.

————. "Gishō, Gangyō Gijaku nado no jōdoron narabini jūnensetsu," *Chūgoku jōdo kyōrishi*, Hōzōkan, 1942, pp. 210-226.

————. *Daijō kishin ron no kenkyū.* Tokyo: Kanao bunen-dō, 1922.

————. "Kishin ron no sennen Amida butsu setsu ni tsuite," *Jōdō gaku*, 13, 1938.

Murakami Senshō. *Bukkyō yuishin ron.* Sōgensha, 1943.

Nagao Gadjin. *Chūkan to Yuishiki.* Tokyo: Iwanami shoten, 1978.

Nakagawa Zenkyō. "Daijō kishin ron ni arawaretaru busshō," *Mikkyō kenkyū*, 73, 1940.

Nakamura Hajime and Kawada Kumatarō, eds. *Kegon shisō.* Kyoto, 1960.

Nakamura Hajime. *Tōyōjin no shii hōhō.* Tokyo, 1948-1949.

Nakayama Nobuji. *Bukkyō ni okeru "toki" no kenkyū.* Kyoto, 1943.

Ninomiya Keinin. "Chōsen ni okeru ninnōe no kaisetsu," *Chōsen gakuhō*, No. 4, 1959, pp. 155-163.

————. "Kōraichō no hakkan'e ni tsuite," *Chōsen gakuhō*, No. 9, 1956, pp. 235-251.

Nukariya Kaiten. "Chōsen zenkyōshi." Tokyo: Shunjūsha, 1930.

Ogawa Ichijō. *Nyoraizō, busshō no kenkyū.* Kyoto, 1969.

Ogawa Jitsugen. "Kishin ron kaishaku no hensen—Kegon kyōgaku tankai no kontei toshite," *Indogaku bukkyōgaku kenkyū*, 13:2, 1965.

Okamoto Sokō. "Hōkai no hitotsu no keitai: kishin ron no shinnyo kan ni tsuite," *Komazawa daigaku bungakubu kenkyū kiyō*, 19, 1961.

————. "Shinnyo gainen no kenkyū: Daijō kishin ron o chūshin to shite, sono ichi danpen," *Komazawa daigaku gakujutsu kenkyū kiyō*, 2, 1967.

————. "Shinri gainen no kōzō—daijō kishin ron ni okeru," *Indogaku bukkyōgaku kenkyū*, 3:2, 1955.

Ōno Hōdō. Tendai to kishinron," *Shūkyō kai*, 10:2-3, 5-6, 1914.

Ota Hisaki. "Shindai sanzō shoyaku ronden ni mirareru nyoraizō," *Indogaku bukkyōgaku kenkyū*, 14:1, 1965.

Ōyama Kojun. "Mumyo to gaku," *Mikkyō bunka*, 32, 1956.

———. "Shujō ni tsuite," *Nihon bukkyō gakkai nempō*, 20, 1955.

Rokuho Kyōjō. "Daijō kishin ron ni okeru shin shometsu ron," *Shūkyō kenkyū*, 142, 1954.

Saigusa, M. "Ryūju ni okeru shin no mondai," in *IBK* III−2 (1954), pp. 297-299.

Sakaino Kōyō. "Daijō kishin ron to daijō kūu nishu no kankei," *Shinbukkyō*, 4:10, 1903.

Sakamoto Yukio. "Genju Daishi no shokan ni tsuite," *Shohon*, No. 62, 1955, pp. 2-4.

———. *Kegon kyōgaku no kenkyū*. Tokyo: Heirakuji, 1964.

Sasaki Kentoku. *Tendai enkiron tankai shi*. Nagada bunshōdō, 1953.

Sekiguchi Shindai. *Daruma Daishi no kenkyū*. Revised edition. Tokyo, 1969.

———. "Goji-hakkyōron," *Tendai gakuhō*, vol. 14, 1972, pp. 12-25.

———. *Tendai shikan no kenkyū*. Tokyo: Iwanami shoten, 1969.

———. *Tendai sho shikan no kenkyū*. Risōsha, 1954.

———. *Zenshū shisōshi*. Tokyo, 1964.

———. "Zenshū to Tendaishū to no kōshō," *Taishō Daigaku kenkyū kiyō*, No. 44, 1959, pp. 39-75.

Shimada Kenji. "Tai-yō no rekishi ni yosete," *Tsukamoto Hakushi shōju kinen Bukkyō shigaku ronshū*. Kyoto, 1961, pp. 416-430.

Shimaji Mokurai. "Kotsujen nenki no kaishaku," *Sanpō sōshi*, 156, 1897.

Shinoda Masahige. "Jishō shōjō shin to prakṛti-prabhasvara," *Hikata hakushi koki kinen ronbunshū*. Tokyo, 1964.

Suzuki Shōgo. "Kishin ron ni okeru mumyo no igi," *Indogaku bukkyōgaku kenkyū*, 1:2, 1953.

Suzuki Shūchū. *Genshi kegon tetsugaku no kenkyū*. Tokyo: Daitō Shuppansha, 1934.

———. "Kishin ron no seiritsu ni kansuru shiryo ni tsuite," *Shūkyo kenkyū* (new series), 5:1-2, 1928.

———. "Kishin ron no seiritsu ni kansuru zairyō," *Bukkyō kenkyū*, 1, 3, 1928.

Taishō shinshū daizōkyō. Tokyo: Daizō shuppan kabushiki kaisha, 1924–1934.

Takahashi Tōru. *Richo bukkyo.* Tokyo: Hōbunkan, 1929.

Takamine Ryōshu. *Kegon shisōshi.* Kyoto: Kōkyō-shoin, 1942.

———. *Hannya to nembutsu, fugen gyōgan bon ronkō.* Kyoto: Nagata bunshōdō, 1950.

———. "Kegon kyō ni okeru fugen-gyōgan-bon no chii," *Ryūkoku daigaku ronshū*, 336, 1949, pp. 1–22.

———. *Kegon to zen tono tsūro.* Nara: Nanto bukkyō kenkyūkai, 1956.

———. "Kishin ron kenkyū no keika," in *Kegon shisō shi.* Kyoto: Hyakukaen, 1942.

Takasaki Jikidō. *Nyoraizō shisō no keisei.* Tokyo: Shunjūsha, 1974.

Takemura Shōhō. *Daijō kishin ron kōdoku.* Kyoto: Hyakukaen, 1959.

———. *Kishin ron nyūmon.* Kyoto: Hyakukaen, 1953.

Tamaki Kōshiro. *Bukkyō no hikaguku shisoronteki kenkyū.* Tokyo: Tokyo Daigaku Shuppankai, 1980.

———. *Chūgoku Bukkyō shisō no keisei*, I. Tokyo, 1971.

Tamura Hōrō. "Bukkyō tetsugaku daikei—daijō kishin ron," *Risō*, 388, 1971.

Tamura Yoshirō. "The New Buddhism of Kamakura and the Concept of Original Enlightenment," *Tōyō University: Asian Studies*, I, 1961.

———, et al. *Zettai no shinri (Bukkyō no shisō* series, No. 5, ed. *Tsukamoto et al.*). Tokyo, 1970.

Tanaka Junshō. "Kishin ron shosetsu no shinnyo," *Nihon bukkyō gakkai nempō*, 8, 1936.

Tokiwa Daijō. *Busshō no kenkyū.* Tokyo, 1944.

———. *Shina Bukkyō no kenkyū*, I-III. Tokyo, 1943.

———. *Shina ni okeru bukkyō to jukyō dōkyō.* Tokyo: Tōyō bunko, 1930.

Tomoki Yokō. "Shoshū no kyōri oyobi kyōhan ni okeru kishin ron no chii," *Ōsaki gakuhō*, 4:30, 1906, 1913.

Tsuda Sōkichi. *Shina Bukkyō no kenkyū.* Tokyo, 1957.

Tsujioka Ryojin. "Guiki no shōsō chōwa shisō ni tsuite (tokuni Daijō kishin ron retsubō so o chūshin to shite)," *Eisan gakuhō,* vol. 12, 1936.

Tsukamoto Zenryū. *Chūgoku Bukkyō tsūshi.* Tokyo, 1942.

———. *Hokuchō bukkyoshi kenkyū (Tsukamoto Zenryū chosakushū,* vol 2). Tokyo: Daitō shuppansha, 1974.

———. ed by, *Jōron kenkyū.* Kyoto, 1955.

———. *Shina Bukkyō shi kenkyū: Hokugi hen.* Tokyo, 1942.

Ueda Yoshifumi. *Bukkyō shisōshi kenkyū: Indo no Daijō Bukkyō.* Kyoto: Nagata Bunshōdō, 1951.

———. "Mōnen ron," included in *Ui ganreki kinen ronshū,* pp. 99-110.

Ui Hakuju. *Bukkyō hanron.* Tokyo, 1949.

———. *Bukkyō shisō kenkyū.* Tokyo: Iwanami shoten, 1943.

———. *Dai san zenshūshi kenkyū.* Tokyo, 1943.

———. *Daijō kishin ron.* Tokyo: Iwanami bunko, 1936. Also in vol. 2 of *Ui Hakuju chōsaku senshū.* Tokyo: Taitō shuppan, 1966.

———. *Hōshōron kenkyū.* Tokyo, 1955.

———. *Shōdaijōron kenkyū.* Tokyo, 1935.

———. tr. by, *Zengen shosenshū tojo.* Tokyo: Iwanami shoten, 1939.

———. *Zenshūshi kenkyū.* Tokyo: Iwanami shoten, 1941.

Yabuki Keiki. *Sangaikyō no kenkyū.* Kyoto, 1927.

Yamada Ryogen. "Nyoraizō-enkishū ni tsuite," *Studies in Indology and Buddhology, presented in honour of Prof. Susumu Yamaguchi,* 1955, pp. 245-253.

———. "Shinnyo suien no shisō ni tsuite," *Indogaku bukkyōgaku kenkyū,* 2:1, 1953.

Yamada Ryūjō. *Daijō Bukkyō seiritsu ron josetsu.* Kyoto, 1959.

Yamaguchi Susumu. *Bukkyō ni okeru mu to u tono tairon.* Kyoto: Kōbundō, 1941.

———. *Hannya shisō shi.* Kyoto: Hōzōkan, 1951.

———. "Kegon-kyo yuishin-ge no indo-teki kunko," *Ōtani gakuhō*, 28:3-4, June 1949, pp. 1-30.

Yamazaki Hiroshi. "Keihō shūmitsu kō," *Ryūkoku shidan*, vols. 56-57, 1967, pp. 104-115.

———. "Keihō Shūmitsu ni tsuite," *Indogaku bukkyōgaku kenkyū*, vol. 15, 1967, pp. 490-495.

———. *Shina chūsei Bukkyō no tenkai*. Tokyo, 1942.

———. *Zui Tō Bukkyō shi no kenkyū*. Kyoto, 1967.

Yanagida Seizan, et al. *Mu no tankyū* (*Bukkyō no shisō* series, No. 7, ed. by, *Tsukamoto et al.*). Tokyo, 1969.

———. *Shoki Zenshū shisho no kenkyū*. Kyoto: Hōzōkan, 1967.

———. *Zen shisō*. Tokyo: Chūkō Shinsho 400, 1975.

Yoshioka Yoshitoyo. *Dōkyō to bukkyō*, vol. 1. Tokyo: Gakujutsu shinkōkai, 1959.

Yoshitani Kakuju. "Mōsō fumbetsu no shiki ika," *Tetsugaku zasshi*, 4:40, 1890.

Yūki Reimon. "Chūgoku bukkyō no keisei," in *Chūgoku no bukkyō* (*Kōza bukkyō*, vol. 4). Tokyo: Ōkura, 1973.

———. "Shina Bukkyō ni okeru mappō shisō no koki," *Tōhō gakuhō*, VI, 1936.

Yutsugi Ryōei. *Kanwa ryōyaku Daijō kishin ron shinshaku*. Hōrinkan, 1914.

IV. Western Sources

Abe, Masao. "Answer to Comment and Criticism," JR 4/2 1966, pp. 26-57.

———. "Buddhism and Christianity as a Problem of Today," JR 3/2, 1963, pp. 11-22; 3/3, pp. 8-31. See also the following "Symposium on Christianity and Buddhism: A Reply to Professor Abe," JR 4/1, 1964, pp. 5-52; 4/2, 1966, pp. 3-25; 8/4 1975, pp. 10-53; 9/1 and 2, 1976.

———. "Christianity and Buddhism—Centering around Science and Nihilism," JR 5/3, 1968, pp. 36-62.

———. "Christianity and the Encounter of the World Religions," EB I/1, 1965, pp. 109-122.

────. "The Crucial Points: An Introduction to the Symposium on Christianity and Buddhism," JR 8/4, 1975, pp. 2-9.

────. "Dōgen on Buddha Nature," EB IV/1, 1971, pp. 28-71.

────. "God, Emptiness, and the True Self," EB II/2, 1969, pp. 15-30.

────. " 'Life and Death' and 'Good and Evil' in Zen," *Criterion*, Autumn, 1969.

────. "Mahayana Buddhism and Whitehead," *PEW* 25, October 1975.

────. "Man and Nature in Christianity and Buddhism," JR 7/1, 1971, pp. 1-10.

────. "Non-Being and *Mu*. The Metaphysical Nature of Negativity in the East and the West," *Religious Studies* II, pp. 181-192.

────. Reading Dr. Nishitani's *What Is Religion?*" *Tetsugaku kenkyū* 42/1, Kyoto, 1962, pp. 83-104.

────. "Religion Challenged by Modern Thought," JR 8/2, 1974, pp. 2-14.

────. "Zen and Compassion," EB II/1, 1967, pp. 54-68.

────. "Zen and Nietzsche," EB VI/2, 1973, pp. 14-32.

────. "Zen to seiyōshisō.,"*Kōza Zen.* ed. by K. Nishitani, Vol. 1, pp. 113-148. English translation: "Zen and Western Thought," *International Philosophical Quarterly* X/4, 1970, pp. 501-541.

Altizer, J. J. Thomas. "Nirvana and the Kingdom of God," *Journal of Religion*, April, 1963, XLIII:2, 105-117.

────. *The Self-embodiment of God.* New York: Harper and Row, 1977.

────. *Total Presence: The Language of Jesus and the Language of Today.* New York: The Seabury Press, 1980.

Anesaki, Masaharu. *History of Japanese Religion.* London: Kegan, Paul, Trench, Trubner & Co., 1930, p. 423.

Ariga Tetsutarō. *The Problem of Ontology in Christian Thought.* Tokyo, 1969.

Bailey, Raymond. *Thomas Merton on Mysticism.* Garden City, New York: Doubleday, 1975.

Banerjee, Anukul Chandra. "Pratītyasamutpāda," *IHQ*, 32, June-Sept., 1956, pp. 261-264.

Barua, B. M. "Faith in Buddhism," in *Buddhistic Studies* (ed. by B. C. Law, Calcutta, 1931), pp. 329-349.

Bendall, C. and de la Vallée Poussin, L. "Bodhisattva-bhūmi. A text book of the Yogācāra school" (An English summary with notes and illustrative extracts from other Buddhistic works). *Muséon* (New Series), VI (1905), pp. 38-52, VII (1906), pp. 213-230, XII (1911), pp. 155-191.

Benz, Ernst. "Mystik als Seinserfüllung bei Meister Eckhart," R. Wisser, pp. 319-413.

————. "Buddhism and Christianity," JR 8/4, 1975, pp. 10-18.

Bhattacharya, V. "Evolution of Vijñānavāda," *JHQ*, X (No. 1), pp. 1-11.

Blakeney, Raymond B. *Meister Eckhart: A Modern Translation.* New York: Harper Torchbooks, 1941.

Blofeld, John, tr. by. *The Zen Teaching of Huang Po: On the Transmission of Mind,* New York: Grove Press 1958.

————. tr. by. *The Zen Teaching of Hui Hai on Sudden Illumination.* New York: Samuel Weiser, 1972.

Bloom, Alfred. *Shinran's Gospel of Pure Grace.* Tucson, Arizona: The University of Arizona Press, 1973.

Bouquet, A. C. *Comparative Religion: A Short Outline.* Baltimore; Penguin Books, 1941.

Broughton, Jeffrey. "Kuei-feng Tsung-mi: The Convergence of Ch'an and the Teachings" (Ph.D. dissertation), Columbia University, 1975.

Bruns, J. Edgar. *The Christian Buddhism of Saint John.* New York: Paulist Press, 1971.

Buber, Martin. *I and Thou.* New York: Charles Scribner's Sons, 1970.

Bucke, Richard Maurice. *Cosmic Consciousness.* New York: E. P. Dutton, 1969.

[181]

Buddhadasa, Indapanno. *Christianity and Buddhism.* Bangkok: Karn Pim Pranakorn, 1967.

Buddhaghosa, Bhadentacariya. *The Path of Purification.* 2 Vols. Translated by Nyanamoli Bhikkhu. Berkeley: Shambhala, 1976.

————. *The Path of Freedom.* Translated by Soma Thera. Colombo: Balcombe House, 1961.

Bultman, Rudolf. *Theology of the New Testament* (tr. by Kendrick Grobel). New York: Charles Scribner's Sons, 1955.

Burton, Naom, et al., ed by. *The Asian Journal of Thomas Merton.* New York: New Directions, 1973.

Casey, David F. *Aspects of the Śūnyatā-Absolute of Nāgārjuna of Second Century A.D. Andhra* (doctoral dissertation) Harvard University, 1960.

————. "Nāgārjuna and Candrakirti. A Study of Significant Differences," *Transactions of the International Conference or Orientalists in Japan* IX, Tōhō Gakkai, Tokyo, 1964, p. 34–45.

Chan, Wing-Tsit. *The Platform Scripture.* New York: St. John's University Press, 1963.

————. *A Source Book in Chinese Philosophy.* Princeton: Princeton University Press, 1973.

Chang, Chung-Yuan. *Original Teachings of Ch'an Buddhism.* New York: Pantheon Books, 1969.

Chang, Garma C. C. *The Buddhist Teaching of Totality: The Philosophy of Hwa-yen Buddhism.* University Park and London: Pennsylvania State University Press, 1971.

Chappell, David W. "Introduction to the *T'ien-t'ai ssu-chiao-i,*" *Eastern Buddhist, New Series,* vol. 9, no. 1, May, 1976, pp. 72–86.

Ch'en, Kenneth. *Buddhism in China: A Historical Survey.* Princeton: Princeton University Press, 1972.

————. *The Chinese Transformation of Buddhism.* Princeton: Princeton University Press, 1973.

Chuck, James. "Zen Buddhism and Paul Tillich: A Comparison of Their Views on Man's Predicament and The

Means of Its Resolution," unpublished Dissertation for Ph.D., Pacific School of Religion, 1962.

Clark, James M. *The Great German Mystic: Eckhart, Tauler and Suso.* Oxford: B. Blackwell, 1949.

————. *Meister Eckhart, An Introduction to the Study of His Works, with An Anthology of His Sermons.* London: Nelson, 1957.

Cleary, Christopher, tr. *Swampland Flowers: The Lectures of Zen Master Ta Hui.* New York: Grove Press, 1977.

Cleary, Thomas and J. C., tr. by. *The Blue Cliff Record.* Boulder, Colorado: Shambhala, 1977.

Cleary, Thomas, tr. by. *Sayings and Doings of Pai-chang.* Los Angeles: Center Publications, 1978.

Cobb, Jr., John B. "Buddhist Emptiness and The Christian God," *Journal of the American Academy of Religion,* March 1977, XLV:1, 11–26.

Collins, W. J. H. "Common Ground in Christianity and Buddhism." *Japanese Religion,* 1972, 7:3, 29–41.

Conze, Edward. *Buddhist Meditation.* New York: Harper and Row, 1969.

————. *Abhisamayālaṅkāra,* S.O.R. 6, IsMEO, Roma, 1954.

————. *Buddhism: Its Essence and Development.* New York: Harper and Row, 1951.

————. *Buddhist Texts Through the Ages.* Oxford, 1954. (tr. of RGV, pp. 130–131, 181–184, 216–217).

————. *Buddhist Thought in China.* Michigan: The University of Michigan Press, 1967.

————. *Buddhist Thought in India. Three Phases of Buddhist Philosophy.* Ann Arbor: University of Michigan Press, 1973.

————. *Vajracchedikā Prajñāpāramitā.* S.O.R. 13, IsMEO, Roma, 1957.

Cook, Francis H. "Causation in the Chinese Hua-yen Tradition: Its Structure and Some Implications." Conference Paper, University of California, Riverside, February, 1976.

[183]

————. "Fa-tsang's Treatise on the Five Doctrines: An Annotated Translation" (Ph.D. dissertation), University of Wisconsin, 1970.

————. *Hua-yen Buddhism: The Jewel Net of Indra.* University Park, Philadelphia: The Pennsylvania State University Press, 1977.

De Bary, William Theodore. *The Buddhist Tradition in India, China, and Japan.* Edited by W. M. Theodore De Bary. New York: Vintage Books Edition, 1972.

————, ed. by. *Sources in Chinese Tradition.* New York: Columbia University Press, 1967.

De Groot, J. J. M. *The Religious System of China,* 6 vols. Taipei: Ch'eng Wen Publishing Co., 1976.

de Jong, J. W. (Review) on J. Takasaki, *A Study on the Ratnagotravibhāga* (Roma, 1966), IIJ 11-1, 1968, pp. 36-54.

————. Review of *Nyoraizō shisō no keisei* by Takasaki Jikidō, *Indo-Iranian Journal,* vol. 18, 1976, pp. 311-315.

De Krester, Bryan, *Man in Buddhism and Christianity.* Calcutta: YMCA Publishing House, 1954.

De Marquette, Jacques. *Introduction to Comparative Mysticism.* New York: Philosophical Library, 1949.

De Martino, Richard Joseph. "The Zen Understanding of Man," unpublished Dissertation for the Ph.D., Temple University, 1969.

Demieville, Paul. "La Penetration du Bouddhisme dans la tradition philosophique chinoise," *Cahiers d'Histoire mondiale,* III, No. 1, 1956.

————. "Sur l'authenticite du Ta tch'eng k'i sin louen." *BMFJ,* Tome II (No. 2, 1929), *Bibliographie Bouddhique,* 11 (No. 122).

————. "La Yogācārabhūmi de Saṅgharaṣka," BEFEO, XLIV, No. 2, 1954, pp. 340-436.

Dempf, Alois, *Meister Eckhart.* Vienna, 1960.

Dewart, Leslie. *The Future of Belief. Theism in a World Come of Age.* New York: Herder and Herder, 1966.

Dudley, Crayton Thomas. "Comparative Religions," *Wilson Library Bulletin.* November 1968, 43:3, 239-247.

Dumoulin, Heinrich, ed. *Buddhism in the Modern World.* London: Collier, 1976.

————. *Christianity Meets Buddhism.* Translated by John C. Maraldo. La Salle, Illinois: Open Court Publishing Company, 1974.

————. *A History of Zen Buddhism.* Boston: Beacon Press, 1971.

Dutt, Nalinaksha. "The Doctrine of Kāya in Hīnayāna and Mahāyāna," *IHQ*, V (No. 3), pp. 518-546.

————. "The Place of the āryasatyas and the pratītyasa-mutpāda in Hīnayāna and Mahāyāna," *ABORI*, XI (Pt. II), pp. 101-127.

————. "Place of Faith in Buddhism," in *Louis de la Vallée Poussin Memorial Volume V* (ed. by Narendra Nath Law, Calcutta, 1940), pp. 421-428.

Dutt, S. *Buddhist Monks and Monasteries of India.* London: George Allen and Unwin, Ltd., 1962.

Eliade, Mircea and Kitagawa Joseph M., eds. *The History of Religions: Essays in Methodology.* Chicago, 1959.

Fenton, John Y. "Buddhist Meditation and Christian Practice," *Anglican Theological Review*, 1971, 53:4, 237-251.

Fernando, Antony. "Salvation and Liberation in Buddhism and in Christianity," *Lumen Vitae*, 1972, 27-2, 304-17.

Fox, Douglas. *Buddhism, Christianity, and the Future of Man.* Philadelphia: The Westminster Press, 1972.

Franck, Frederick, ed. by. *The Buddha Eye: An Anthology of The Kyoto School.* New York: The Crossroad Publishing Company, 1982.

————. compiled by. *Zen and Zen Classics: Selections from R. H. Blyth.* New York: Vintage Books, 1978.

Frauwallner, E. "Amalvigñānam and Ālayavijñānam. Ein Beitrag zur Erkenntnislehre des Buddhismus," *BIPA*, pp. 148-159.

Fromm, Erich, Suzuki, D. T., and De Martino, Richard. *Zen Buddhism and Psychoanalysis.* New York: Harper Colophon Books, 1970.

Fung, Yu-lan. *A History of Chinese Philosophy*. Vol. 11. Translated by Derk Bodde. Princeton: Princeton University Press, 1953.

Gard, Richard A. "The Mahdyamika in Korea," in *Paek Song-uk Paksa Songsu Kinyom Bulgyohak Nonmunjip*. Seoul, 1959.

Gimello, Robert M. "Apophatic and kataphatic discourse in Mahayana: A Chinese View," *Philosophy East and West*, Vol. 26, No. 2, April, 1976, pp. 117–136.

————. "Chih-yen and the Foundations of Hua-yen Buddhism." (Ph.D. dissertation), Columbia University, 1976.

Gnoli, R. (Review) on J. Takasaki, *A Study on the RGV* (Roma, 1966), RSO 41-3, pp. 276–277.

Gokhale, V. V. A Note on Ratnagotravibhāga I, 52 — Bhagavadgītā XIII, 32, *Studies in Indology and Buddhology*, Presented in Honour of Professor Susumu Yamaguchi on the Occasion of his Sixtieth Birthday. Kyoto, 1955, pp. 90–91.

Govinda, Anagarika. *The Psychological Attitude of Early Buddhist Philosophy and Its Systematic Representation According to Abhidhamma Tradition*. New York: S. Weiser, 1969.

Graham, A. C. "Chuang Tzu's Essay on Seeing Things as Equal," *History of Religions*, vol. 9, nos. 2 and 3, November 1969–December 1970, PP. 137–159.

————. *The Book of Lieh Tzu*. London: John Murray, 1960.

————. *Two Chinese Philosophers: Ch'eng Ming-tao and Ch'eng Yi-ch'uan*. London: Lund Humphries, 1967.

Gregory, Peter Nielson. *Tsung-mi's Inquiry into the Origin of Man: A Study of Chinese Buddhist Hermeneutics* (Ph.D. Dissertation). Cambridge: Harvard University, 1981.

Hakeda, Yoshito S. *The Awakening of Faith*, attributed to Aśvaghosa, translated with commentary. New York: Columbia University Press, 1967.

Han, Ki-bum. "Zen and The Bible: A Study of D. T. Suzuki's Dialogue with Christianity," (Ph. D. dissertation), Temple University, 1975.

Hare, E. M., tr. by. *The Book of Gradual Sayings*, 5 vols. London: Pali Text Society 1961-1972.

Hashimoto,Hideo. "The Christian Faith and Jodo-Shin Buddhism," *Occasional Papers*, 6, July 1960, International Missionary Council, p. 14.

Hattori Masaaki. Review of *La Theorie du Tathāgata et du Gotra* by David Seyforth Ruegg, *Journal of Indian Philosophy*, vol. 2, no. 1, 1972, pp. 53-64.

Herrigel, Eugen. *Zen in the Art of Archery*. New York: Random House, 1971.

Hirabayashi, Jay and Shotaro Iida. "Another Look at the Mādhyamika vs. Yogācāra Controversy Concerning Existence and Non-existence," in Lewis Lancaster, ed., *Prajñāpāramitā and Related Systems: Studies in Honor of Edward Conze*. Berkeley: Berkeley Buddhist Studies, 1977, pp. 341-368.

Hirakawa, A. The Rise of Mahāyāna Buddhism and Its Relationship to the Worship of Stūpas, *Memoirs of the Research Department of the Toya Bunko*, 22, 1963, pp. 57-106.

Hisamatsu Shin'ichi. "The Characteristics of Oriental Nothingness," PSJ II, 1960, pp. 65-97.

————. "Zen: Its Meaning for Modern Civilization," EB I/1, 1965, pp. 22-47.

————*Works*: Vol. 2, *The Way of Absolute Subjectivity*; Vol. 3, *Awakening and Creativity*; Vol. 5, *Zen to geijutsu*. English translation, *Zen and the Fine Arts*, Tokyo, 1971.

————. "Ultimate Crisis and Resurrection," EB VIII/1, 1975, pp. 12-29; VIII/2, pp. 37-65.

————. "Kishin no kadai (The Problems of the Awakening of Faith)," *Tetsugaku kenkyū, The Journal of Philosophical Studies*, Kyoto University, 1946, No. 354, pp. 20-45; No. 355, pp. 18-37.

Hoffman, Yoel, tr. by. *The Sound of the One Hand*. New York: Basic Books, 1975.

Honda, Masaaki. "The Buddhist Logic of 'Soku' and Christianity," *Katorikku kenkyū XII/1*, 1973, pp. 1-25.

Horner, I. B., *The Middle Length Sayings*, 3 vols. London: Pali Text Society, 1975-1977.

Humphreys, Christmas. *The Wisdom of Buddha*. New York: Random House, 1961, p. 280.

Hsüan-hua, commentary by. *Flower Adornment Sutra*, Talmage, California: The Buddhist Text Translation Society, 1980.

―――. *Dharma Flower Sutra*. Talmage, California, 1980.

Hurvitz, Leon. *Chih-i: An Introduction to the Life and Ideas of a Chinese Buddhist Monk*. Brussells: L'Institut Belge des Hautes Études Chinoises, 1962.

――― and Tsukamoto Zenryū. *Wei Shou, Treatise on Buddhism and Taoism*. Kyoto: Jimbunkagaku kenkyūsho, 1956.

Hu, Shih. "Ch'an (Zen) Buddhism in China, Its History and Method," *Philosophy East and West*, III, No. 1, 1953, pp. 3-24.

―――. "Development of Zen Buddhism in China," *Chinese Social and Political Science Review*, XV, 1931.

―――. "The Indianization of China: A Case Study in Cultural Borrowings," *Independence, Convergence and Borrowing in Institutions, Thought and Art*. Cambridge, Mass., 1937.

Ignatius, Saint. *The Spiritual Exercises of St. Ignatius*. Translated by Mottola, Anthony. Garden City, New York: Image Books, 1964.

Inada, Kenneth K. "The Metaphysics of Buddhist Experience and the Whiteheadian Encounter," *PEW* 25, October 1975.

―――. *Nagarjuna: A translation of his Mūlamadhyamakakārika*. Tokyo: The Hokuseido Press, 1970.

Inoue, Eiji et al. (eds.). *A Dialogue of Religions: Christianity and the Religions of Japan*. Tokyo, 1973.

James, E. O. *Comparative Religion*. New York: Barnes and Nobel, 1961.

James, William. *Varieties of Religious Experience*. New York: Coller Books, 1970.

Jan Yün-hua. "Conflict and Harmony in Ch'an and Buddhism," *Journal of Chinese Philosophy*, vol. 4, no. 3,

1977, pp. 287-301.

————. "Tsung-mi: His Analysis of Ch'an Buddhism," *T'oung Pao*, vol. 58, 1972, pp. 1-53.

————. "Tsung-mi's Questions Regarding the Confucian Absolute," *Philosophy East and West*, vol. 30, 1980, pp. 495-504.

Johansson, Runne. *The Psychology of Nirvana*. London: George Allen and Unwin Ltd., 1969.

Johnston, E. H. and Chowdhury, T. "The Ratnagotravibhāga Mahāyānottaratantraśāstra." *JBORS*, 36, 1950, Appendix, i-xvi, pp. 1-129.

Johnston, William. *Christian Zen*. New York: Harper Colophone Books, 1974.

————. Edited. *The Cloud of Unknowing*. Garden City, New York: Image Books, 1973.

————. *The Still Point. Reflections on Zen and Christian Mysticism*. New York: Harper and Row, 1971.

Jordan, Louise Henry. *Comparative Religion, Its Adjuncts and Allies*. London: Oxford University Press, 1915.

Kadowaki, Kakichi. "Ways of Knowing," A Buddhist-Thomist Dialogue, *Japanese Missionary Bulletin* XIII/8, 1969, pp. 467-474; XXIII/9, pp. 515-530.

————. "Towards a Better Understanding of Zen Buddhism," *Japanese Missionary Bulletin* XXIII/10, 1969, pp. 611-619.

————. "A Review of Honda's Article on 'Soku' ", Katorikku Kenkyū XII/2, 1973, pp. 153-159; a continuation of the discussion appears *Ibid.*, XIII/2, 1974, pp. 149-172.

————. *The Ignation Exercises and Zen. An Attempt at Synthesis*. Jersey City, N.J., 1974.

Kalupahana, David J. *Buddhist Philosophy*. Honolulu: The University Press of Hawaii, 1970.

————. *Causality: The Central Philosophy of Buddhism*. Honolulu: The University Press of Hawaii, 1975.

Kapleau, Philip. *The Three Pillars of Zen, Teachings, Practice, Enlightenment*. Garden City, New York: Anchor Books, 1980.

Keel, Hee Sung. *Chinul, the Founder of Korean Sŏn (Zen) Tradition.* (Ph.D. Thesis) Cambridge, Mass.: Harvard University, April 1977.

Kim, Hee Jin. *Dōgen Kigen-mystical Realist.* Tucson: The University of Arizona Press, 1975.

King, Winston L. *Buddhism and Christianity. Some Bridges of Understanding.* London, 1962.

———. "East-West Religious Communication," EB I/2, 1966, pp. 91-110.

———. "Śūnyatā as a Master-Symbol," *Numen* XVII, Leiden, 1970, pp. 95-104.

———. "The Impersonal Personalism and Subjectivism of Buddhist 'Nihilism,' " JR 8/4, 1975, pp. 37-53.

Kitagawa, Joseph M. *Religion in Japanese History.* New York, 1966.

Kiyota Minoru. "The Structure and Meaning of Tendai Thought," *Transactions of the International Conference of Orientalists in Japan,* vol. 5, 1960, pp. 69-83.

Kreeft, Peter. "Zen Buddhism and Christianity: An Experiment in Comparative Religion," *Journal of Ecumenical Studies,* 1971, 8:3, 513-538.

Kunii, Paul. "Buddhism in Christian Perspective," *Thought.* Autumn 1965, XL:158, pp. 390-414.

Lai, Whalen Wai-lun. *The Awakening of Faith in Mahāyāna (Ta-ch'eng ch'i-hsin lun): A Study of the Unfolding of Sinitic Mahāyāna Motifs.* (Ph.D. Thesis). Cambridge Mass.: Harvard University, August, 1975.

———. "Further Development of the Two Truths Theory in China: The Ch'eng-shih-lun Tradition and Chou Yung's San-tsung-lun," *PEW* 30, April, 1980.

Lamotta, Étienne, trs. *L'Enseignement de Vimalakīrti (Vimalakīrtinirdeśa).* Louvain: Publications Universitaires and Leuven: Institut Orientaliste, 1962.

———. trs. *Samdhinirmocana Sūtra: L'Explication des mystères. Louvain: Universite de Louvain,* 1935.

———. *La Somme du Grand Véhicule d'Asaṅga (Mahāyānasaṃghraha).* Louvain: Bureau du Muséon, 1938-1939.

———, trs. *Le Traité de la Grande Virtu De Sagesse de*

Nāgārjuna (Mahāprajñāpāramitāśāstra). Louvain: Publications Universitaires and Leuven: Institut Orientaliste, 1949.

Lassalle, H. M. Enomiya. *Zen Meditation for Christians*. La Salle, Ill.: Open Court, 1974.

Lee, Peter H. "Fa-tsang and Ŭisang," *Journal of the American Oriental Socitey*, LXXXII, No. 1, 1962, pp. 56–62.

———. *Lives of Eminent Korean Monks: The Haedong Kosŭng Chŏn*. Cambridge, Mass., 1969.

Lessing, F. D. "The Thirteen Visions of a Yogācārya. A preliminary study." *Ethnos*, Nos. 3-4, 1950, pp. 108–130.

Lévi, Sylvain. *Asaṅga; Mahāyāna-Sūtrālaṃkāra, Exposé de la doctrine du Grand Véhicule selon le système Yogācāra*. Paris: Champion, 1907-1911.

Liebenthal, Walter. *The Book of Chao*. Peking, 1948.

———. "The Immortality of the Soul in Chinese Thought," *Monumenta Nipponica*, vol. 8, 1952, pp. 327–397.

———. "New Light on the Mahāyāna Śraddhotpāda Śāstra," *T'ong Pao*, XLVI, Leiden, 1958, pp. 155–216.

———. Notes on the "Vajrasamādhi," TP 44, 1956.

———. "World Conception of Chu Tao-shung," MN 12/1-2, 1956.

Link, Arthur. "Shyh Daw-an's Preface to Saṅgharaska's Yogācārabhūmisūtra and the Problem of Buddho-Taoist Terminology in Early Chinese Buddhism," *JAOS*, 77, No. 1, 1957, pp. 1–14.

———. and Tim Lee. "Sun Ch'o's *Yü-tao-lun: A Clarification of the Way*," *Monumenta Serica*, vol. 25, 1966, pp. 169–196.

Liu, Ming-wood, "The Teaching of Fa-tsang: An Examination of Buddhist Metaphysics" (Ph.D. dissertation), University of California at Los Angeles, 1979.

Luk, Charles, trs. *The Vimalakirti Nirdesa Sutra*. Berkeley and London: Shambala, 1972.

Lu, K'uan-Yu (Charles Luk). *The Secrets of Chinese Meditation*. London, 1964.

Masson-Oursel, Paul. "Tathāgatagarbha et Ālayavijñāna," *JA*, CCX, 1927, pp. 295–302.

Masunaga, Reihō. *The Sōtō Approach to Zen*. Tōkyō: Laymen Buddhist Society Press, 1958, p. 215.

Masutani, Fumio. *A Comparative Study of Buddhism and Christianity*. Tokyo: Bukkyo Dendo Kyokai, 1967.

Mather, Richard. "The Conflict of Buddhism with Native Chinese Ideologies," *The Review of Religion*, vol. 20, 1955, pp. 25-37.

————. "The Controversy over Conformity and Naturalism during the Six Dynasties," *History of Religions*, IX, 1969.

Matsunaga, Alicia. *The Buddhist Philosophy of Assimilation. The Historical Development of the Honji-Suijaku Theory*, Tokyo, 1969.

May, J. (Review) on D. Seyfort Ruegg. *La Théorie du tathāgatagarbha et du gotra*. Paris, 1971, TP 57, pp. 147-157.

Merton, Thomas, *The Ascent to Truth*. New York, 1951.

————. *Mysticism and Zen Masters*. New York, 1967.

————. *Basic Principles of Monastic Spirituality*. Bardstown, Kentucky: Abbey of Gethsemani, 1957.

————. "Contemplation and Ecumenism," *Season*, Fall, 1965, 3:3, 133-142.

————. "The Contemplative and the Atheist," *Schema* XIII, January, 1970, 1:1, 11-18.

————. *Contemplative Prayer*. New York: Image Books, 1971.

————. *Faith and Violence: Christian Teaching and Christian Practice*. Notre Dame, Indiana: University of Notre Dame Press, 1968.

————. *Gandhi on Non-violence*. Edited with an Introduction by Thomas Merton. New York: New Directions, 1965.

————. "Meditation: Action and Union," *Sponsa Regis*, March, 1960, 31:7, 291-298.

————. *Mystics and Zen Masters*. New York: Farrar, Straus and Giroux, 1967.

————. *No Man Is An Island*. New York: Image Books, 1967.

———. "Notes on Contemplation," *Spiritual Life*. Fall, 1961, 7:3, pp. 196–202.

———. *Opening the Bible*. Collegeville, Min.: Liturgical Press, 1970.

———. *Original Child Bomb: Points for Meditation to be Scratched on the Wall of a Cave*. New York: New Directions, 1962.

———. *The Tower of Babel*. Norfolk, Conn.: New Directions, 1958.

———. *The True Solitude*. Selections from Thomas Merton's writings by Dean Walley. Kansas City, Missouri: Hallmark Productions, 1969.

———. *The Way of Chuang Tzu*. New York: New Directions, 1965.

———. *What Is Contemplation?* London: Burns Oates and Washbourne, 1950.

———. *Zen and the Birds of Appetite*. New York: New Directions, 1968.

Miller, Ed. L., ed. by. *Classical Statements on Faith and Reason*. New York: Random House, 1970.

Miura, Isshū et al. *The Zen Koan: Its History and Use in Rinzai Zen*. New York: Harvest Book, 1965.

Miyuki, Mokusen. "An Analysis of Buddhist Influence on the Formation of the Sung Confucian Concept of 'Li-Chi.' " (Ph.D. dissertation), Department of Religion, Claremont Graduate School, 1964.

Mohler, James A. *Dimensions of Faith*. Chicago: Loyola University Press, 1969.

Mookerjee, Satkari. *The Buddhist Philosophy of Universal Flux*. Delhi: Motilal Banaesidass, 1980.

Morgan, Kenneth, ed. by. *The Path of Buddha*. New York: Ronald Press, 1956, p. 432.

Müller, F. Max, ed. by. *Sacred Books of the East*, Vol. XXI. Oxford: Clarendon Press, 1884, p. 454.

Murti, T. R. V., *The Central Philosophy of Buddhism. A Study of the Mādhyamika System*. London: Allen and Unwin, 1970.

Nagao, G. M. "Connotations of the word *āśraya* (basis)

in the Mahāyānasūtrālaṅkāra," Liebenthal Festschrift, May 1957, pp 147-155.

Nakamura, Hajime. "The Influence of Confucian Ethics on the Chinese Translations of Buddhist Sutras," *Sino-Indian Studies*, 5: Nos. 3-4, 1957.

————. *Ways of Thinking of the Eastern People*. Edited by Phillip P. Wiener. Honolulu: An East-West Center Book, 1970.

Needham, Joseph. *Science and Civilization in China*, II, Cambridge, Great Britain, 1956.

Nishida, Kitarō. *Complete Works*, 18 vols., Tokyo, 1947-1953; new edition, 1965.

Nishitani, Keiji, *Shūkō towa Nanika*. Tokyo: Sōbunsha, 1961. The English translation, insofar as it has been published: Ch. 1, "What is Religion?" PSJ II, Tokyo, 1960, pp. 21-64; Ch. 2, "The Personal and the Impersonal in Religion," EB III/1, 1970, pp. 1-18; III/2, pp. 71-88; Ch. 3, "Nihilism and Śūnyatā," EB IV/2, 1971, pp. 30-49; V/1, 1972, pp. 55-69; V/2, pp. 95-106; Ch. 4, "The Standpoint of Śūnyatā," EB VI/1, 1973, pp. 68-91; VI/2, pp. 58-86; Ch. 5, "Emptiness and Time," EB IX/1, 1976, pp. 42-71; X/2, 1977, pp. 1-30.

————."Towards a Philosophy of Religion with the Concept of Pre-Established Harmony as Guide," EB III/1, 1970, pp. 19-46.

———— "The Problem of Time in Shinran," *Shinran Zenshū* (Gendaigoyaku), Vol. 10, Tokyo, 1958, pp. 76-86. English translation: EB XI/1, 1978, pp. 13-26.

————. "Science and Zen," EB I/1, 1965, pp. 79-108.

————. "The Awakening of Self in Buddhism," EB I/2, 1966, pp. 1-11.

————. *Lectures on Zen*, ed., 8 vols., Tokyo, 1967-1968.

————, with R. Mutai et al. *What Is Philosophy?* Tokyo, 1967.

————. *Gendai Nippon Shisōtaikei No. 2*, ed., Tokyo, 1968.

————. "A Buddhist Philosopher Looks at the Future of Christianity," *The Japan Christian Yearbook*, Tokyo, 1968, pp. 108-111.

————. "On the I-Thou Relationship in Zen Buddhism," EB II/2, 1969, pp. 71-87.

Noda, Matao. "East-West Synthesis in Kitarō Nishida," *Philosophy East and West*. Hawaii, 1954-1955, pp. 345-359.

Obata, Yoshinobu. "Japanese Buddhism and Its Problems, Seen in the Light of Modern Christian Theological Methodology," *Katorikku kenkyū*, XIII/2, 1974, pp. 78-102.

Obermiller, E. "The Doctrine of Prajñāpāramitā as exposed in the Abhisamayālaṃkāra of Maitreya," *Acta Orientalia*, XI, 1932, pp. 1-181, 334-354.

————. *The Sublime Science of the Great Vehicle to Salvation, Being a Manual of Buddhist Monism*, AO 9-3, 4, 1931, pp. 81-306. Reprint, Shanghai, 1940.

Odin, Steve. *Process Metaphysics and Hua-yen Buddhism: A Critical Study of Cumulative Penetration vs. Interpenetration*. Albany: State University of New York Press, 1982.

Ogden, Schubert M., tr. by. *Existence and Faith: Shorter Writings of Rudolf Bultmann*. New York: Meridian Books, 1966.

————. *Faith and Freedom: Toward a Theology of Liberation*. Nashville: Abdingdon, 1979.

Oh, Kang Nam. "A Study of Chinese Hua-yen Buddhism with Special Reference to the *Dharmadhātu (Fa-chieh)* Doctrine" (Ph.D. Dissertation), McMaster University, 1976.

————. "*Dharmadhātu*: An Introduction to Hua-yen Buddhism," *Eastern Buddhist, New Series*, vol. 12, no. 2, October 1979, pp. 72-91.

Otto, Rudolf. *The Idea of the Holy*. London: Oxford University Press, 1971.

————. *Mysticism East and West*. New York: Macmillan Company, 1972.

Park, Sung-bae. "A Comparative Study of Wŏnhyo and Fa-tsang on the Ta'-ch'eng Ch'i-hsin lun," *Proceedings in the First International Conference of Korean Studies.* Seoul: The Academy of Korean Studies, 1980, pp. 579-597.

————. "The Impact of Buddhism on the Axiological System Underlying Korean Culture," *Proceedings in the Symposium of Religions in Korea: Beliefs and Cultural Values.* California State University, Los Angeles, October 15-18, 1980.

————. "Korean Monk Chinul's Theory of Sudden Enlightenment and Gradual Practice," *Asian Culture,* vol. VIII, No. 4, Taiwan, 1980.

————. "Simile of Water and Waves in Buddhism," *Festschrift for Dr. Dong-shik Rhee.* Seoul, 1981.

————. *Wŏnhyo's Commentaries on the Awakening of Faith in Mahāyāna* (Ph.D. Dissertation), University of California at Berkeley, 1979.

————. "On Wŏnhyo's Enlightenment," *Journal of Indian and Buddhist Studies,* Vol. XXIX, No. 1, Japan, December 1980.

————. "Zen and Pure Land in Korea," *Young Buddhist,* Malaysia, 1981.

Paul, Diana. *The Buddhist Feminine Ideal: Queen Śrīmālā and the Tathāgatagarbha* (American Academy of Religion Dissertation Series No. 30). Missoula, Montana: Scholars Press, 1980.

Pratt, James B. "Korean Buddhism," *The Pilgrimage of Buddhism and a Buddhist Pilgrimage.* New York, 1928.

Prebish, Charles. *Buddhist Monastic Disciple.* University Park and London: Pennsylvania State University Press, 1975.

Radhakrishnan, S. *Eastern Religions and Western Mind.* London: Oxford University Press, 1969.

————. *Recovery of Faith.* New Delhi: Orient Paperbacks, 1967.

Reischauer, E. O. and Fairbank, J. K. *East Asia: The Great Tradition.* Boston, 1960.

Rhys Davids, T. W. and C. A. F., tr. by. *Dialogues of the Buddha*, 3 vols. (*Sacred Books of the Buddhists*, vols. 2-4). London: Pali Text Society, 1977.

Rhys Davids, T. W. and Hermann Oldenberg, tr. by. *Vinaya Texts*, 3 vols. (*The Sacred Books of the East*, vols. 13, 17, and 20). Oxford: Oxford University Press, 1881.

Richard, Timothy (Rev.). *The Awakening of Faith in the Mahāyāna Doctrine*. Shanghai: Christian Literature Society, 1907.

———. *The New Testament of Higher Buddhism. Being a New Trans. of the Saddharma Puṇḍarika and the Mahāyāna-śraddhotpāda śāstra*. New York: Scribner, 1910.

Robinson, Richard H. tr. by. *The Awakening of Faith in Mahāyāna*. (Unpublished manuscript)

———. *Early Mādhyamika in India and China*. Madison, Wisconsin, 1967.

Ruegg, David S. "Le Dharmadhātustava de Nāgārjuna, *Études Tibétaines*, dédiées à la mémoire de Marcelle Lalou, Paris, 1971, pp. 448-471.

———. "On the Knowability and Expressibility of Absolute Reality in Buddhism." *JIBS*, XX (No. 1, 1971), pp. 489-495.

———. *La Théorie du Tathāgatagarbha et du Gotra: Étude sur la Sotériologie et la Gnoséologie du Bouddhisme*. Paris. École Française d'Extrême-Orient, 1969.

———. *Le Traité du Tathāgatagarbha de Bu ston rin chen grub* (Traduction de De bžin gšegs pa'i sñiṅ po gsal žin mdzes par byed pa'i rgyan). Publ. ÉFEO 88, Paris, 1973.

Ryan, John K., tr. by. *The Confessions of St. Augustine*. Garden City, New York: Image Books, 1960.

Sasaki, Ruth Fuller, et al., tr. by. *The Recorded Sayings of Layman P'ang*. New York: Weatherhill, 1971.

Sekida, Katsuki, tr. by. *Two Zen Classics: Mumonkan and Hekiganroku*. New York: Weatherhill, 1977.

Shibayama, Zenkei. *Zen Comments on the Mumonkan* (the

authoritative translation, with commentary, of a basic Zen text). New York, 1974.

Shimomura, Toratarō. *Nishida Kitarō: The Man and His Thought*. Tokyo, 1965.

———. "Nishida Kitarō and Some Aspects of His Philosophical Thought," *Nishida. A Study of the Good*, pp. 191–217.

Shin, Ock Hee. "Man in Wŏnhyo and Karl Jaspers," *Korea Journal* 17, no. 10, October 1977.

Stcherbatsky, Th. "The Dharmas of the Buddhist and the 'Guṇas' of the Sāṃkhyas," *IHQ*, X (No. 4), pp. 737–760.

Steffney, John. "Compassion in Mahāyāna Buddhism and Meister Eckhart," *Journal of Religious Thought*, 1974–1975, 31:2, pp. 64–77.

Streeter, Canon B. H. *The Buddha and the Christ*. London: Macmillan and Company, 1932.

Streng, Frederick J. *Emptiness. A Study in Religious Meaning*. New York, 1967.

———. "Metaphysics, Negative Dialectic, and the Expression of the Inexpressible," *PEW* 25, October, 1979.

Suh, Kyung Soo and Kim, Chul Choon. "Korean Buddhism: A Historical Perspective," in *Buddhist Culture in Korea*. Korean Culture Series 3. General editor Chun Shin-yong. Seoul: International Foundation, 1974.

Sun, George C. "Chinese Metaphysics and Whitehead." Ph.D. dissertation, Department of Religion, Southern Illinois University, 1971.

Suzuki, D. T. *Açvaghosha's Discourse on the Awakening of Faith in the Mahāyāna (Daijōkishinron)*. Chicago: Open Court Publishing Company, 1900.

———. *Essays in Zen Buddhism*. 3 vols. New York, 1961.

———. "Zen: A Reply to Hu Shih," *Philosophy East and West*, III, No. 1, 1953, pp. 25–46.

———. *The Zen Doctrine of No Mind: The Significance of the Sūtra of Hui-neng (Wei-lang)*. New York, 1973.

———. *Zen and Japanese Culture*. Princeton University Press, 1970.

————. *Introduction to Zen Buddhism.* New York, 1949.

————. "On the Hekiganroku (The Blue Cliff Record)," EB I/1, 1965, pp. 5-21; cf. I/2, 1966, pp. 12-20.

————. *Zenshū: Complete Works,* 31 vols., Tokyo, 1968-1970.

————. "Self the Unattainable," EB III/2, 1970, pp. 1-8.

————. "Infinite Light," EB IV/2, 1971, pp. 1-29.

————. "The Seer and the Seen," EB V/1, 1972, pp. 1-25.

————. *Mysticism: Christian and Buddhist.* New York: Harper and Row, 1957.

————. "Zen Buddhism and a Commonsense World," EB VII/1, 1974, pp. 1-18.

————. "The Buddhist Conception of Reality," EB VII/2, 1974, pp 1-21. N.B.: For further bibliographical information on the works of Suzuki, see H. Rzepkowski, *Das Menshenbild bei Daisetz Teitaro Suzuki*, St. Augustine, 1971, pp. viii-xii; EB II/1, 1967, pp. 216-229; III/2, 1970, pp. 146ff.

———— and T. N. Callaway. "A Dialogue," EB III/1, 1970, pp. 109-122.

———— and S. Ueda. "The Sayings of Rinzai," EB VI/1, 1973, pp. 92-110.

————. "Laṅkāvatāra Sūtra, as a Mahāyāna text in special relation to the teaching of Zen Buddhism," EB, IV, October 1927-March 1928, pp 199-298.

————. "Notes on the Avataṃsaka Sūtra," EB, I, 1921-1922, pp. 233-236.

————. "Philosophy of the Yogācāra. The Mādhyamika and the Yogācāra," *Muséon* (New Series), V, 1904, pp. 370-386.

————. *Studies in the Laṅkāvatārasūtra, one of the most important texts of Mahāyāna Buddhism, in which all its principle tenets are presented, including the teaching of Zen.* London: George Routledge, 1930.

Suzuki, Shunryū. *Zen Mind Beginner's Mind.* New York: Weatherhill, 1976.

Swearer, Donald. "Three Modes of Zen in America," *Journal of Ecumenical Studies*, 1973, 10:2, pp. 290-303.

Takakusu, Junjirō. *The Essentials of Buddhist Philosophy*. Honolulu, 1956.

Takasaki, Jikidō. "Buddhist Concept of the Spiritual Family," *Buddhist Annual* 2511-1967, Colombo, 1967, pp. 94-97.

————. "Description of the Ultimate Reality in Mahāyāna Buddhism — by Means of the Six Categories Beginning with *svabhāva*," *JIBS* 9-2, March 1961, pp. 740-731.

————. Dharmatā, Dharmadhātu, Dharmakāya and Buddhadhātu — Structure of the Ultimate Value in Mahāyāna Buddhism, JIBS 14-2, March 1966, pp. 919-903.

————. *A Study on the Ratnagotravibhāga (Uttaratantra) Being a Treatise on the Tathāgatagarbha Theory of Mahāyāna Buddhism*, S.O.R. 33, IsMEO, Roma, 1966.

————. "The Tathāgatagarbha Theory in the Mahā parinirvāṇasūtra," JIBS 19-2, March 1971, pp. 1024-1015.

Takeda, Ryusei, and Cobb, John B., Jr. "Mosa-Dharma' and Prehension: Nagarjuna and Whitehead Compared," *Process Studies* 4 (1974).

Takeuchi, Yoshinori. "The Basic Motivation for Speculation in the Doctrine of Pratītyasamutpāda," *A Festschrift for Dr. Yamaguchi on Indian Buddhism*, Kyoto, 1955, pp. 136-144.

————. "Buddhism and Existentialism: The Dialogue between Oriental and Occidental Thought," W. Leibrecht, ed., *Religion and Culture: Essays in Honor of Paul Tillich*, New York, 1959, pp. 291-365.

————. "Buddhism and Nihilism," *Kōzakindaibukkyō*, Vol. 3, Kyoto, 1962, pp. 72-103.

————. "The Enlightenment of the Buddha," *Chūōkōron* 89/5, 1974, pp. 300-310.

————. "Hegel and Buddhism,"*Il Pensiero* VII/1-2, 1962, pp. 5-46.

————. "The Problem of Dependency in the Doctrine of Pratītyasamutpāda," A Collection of Essays Commemorating the 50th Anniversary of the Faculty of Letters of Kyoto University, Kyoto, 1956, pp. 153-181.

―――. "The Philosophy of Nishida," JR 3/4, 1963, pp. 1-32.

Takizawa, Katsumi. "Was hindert mich noch, mich taufen zu lassen?: Antwort," *K. Barth zum 70. Geburtstag am 10.5.1956*, Zollikon, 1956, pp. 911-925.

―――. "Buddhism and Christianity," Kyoto, 1964.

Tamaki, Kōshirō. "The Absolute in Mahāyāna Buddhism— Possible Conditions of Our Understanding," JIBS 13-1, January 1965, pp. 1-8.

―――. "The Development of Thought of Tathāgatagarbha from India to China." *IBK*, 9, January 1961, pp. 386-378.

Thomas, Edward J. *The History of Buddhist Thought.* New York: Barnes and Noble, Inc., 1971.

Thurman, Robert A. F. "Buddhist Hermeneutics," *Journal of the American Academy of Religion*, vol 49, no. 1, 1978, pp. 19-39.

―――. trans. *The Holy Teaching of Vimalakīrti.* University Park, Philadelphia: The Pennsylvania State University Press, 1976.

Tillich, Paul. *Christianity and the Encounter of the World Religions.* New York: Columbia University Press, 1963.

―――. *Dynamics of Faith.* New York: Harper & Row, 1957.

Toynbee, Arnold Joseph. *Christianity Among the Religions of the World.* New York: Scribner's Sons, 1957.

Tsujimura, Kōichi. "Dialectics and Time," *Tetsugaku Kenkyū* XLII/7, 1964, pp. 645-660.

―――. "Bultmann and Heidegger: Belief and Thought," *Tetsugaku kenkyū*, XLII/11, pp. 1031-1050.

Tucci, G. "Notes on Laṅkāvatāra." *IHQ*, IV (No. 3, 1928).

Ueda Shizuteru. *Die Gottesgeburt in der Seele und der Durchbruch zur Gottheit. Die mystische Anthropologie Meister Eckharts und ihre Konfrontation mit der Mystik des Zen-Buddhismus.* Gütersloh, 1965.

―――. "Der Buddhismus und das Problem der Säkularisierung. Zur gegenwärtigen geistigen Situation Japans," O. Schatz, ed., *Hat die Religion Zukunft?* Cologne, 1971, pp. 255–275.

―――. *Zen Buddhism.* Original Man. Tokyo, 1973.

Ueda, Yoshifumi. "Two Main Streams in Yogācāra Philosophy," *Philosophy East and West*, vol. 17, 1967, pp. 155–165.

Ui, Hakuju. *A Concise Dictionary of Buddhism.* Tokyo, 1953.

Unno, Taitetsu. "The Buddhatā Theory of Fa-tsang." International Conference of Orientalists in Japan. Transactions no. 8 (1963), pp. 34–41.

―――. "The Dimensions of Practice in *Hua Yen* Thought," *Bukkyō shisō shi ronshū.* Tokyo, 1964.

Verdu, Alfonso. *Dialectical Aspects in Buddhist Thought: Studies in Sino-Japanese Mahāyāna Idealism.* Center for East Asian Studies, University of Kansas, 1974.

Vial, Alfred. "The Identity of Saṃsāra and Nirvāṇa," *The Middle Way, Journal of the Buddhist Society*, February, 1971, 451:4, pp. 163–173.

Wach, Joachim. *The Comparative Study of Religions.* New York: Columbia University Press, 1958.

Wai-tao and Goddard, Dwight trans. "The Awakening of Faith in Mahāyāna," *A Buddhist Bible*, ed. Goddard. New York, 1952.

Wadenfels, Hans. "Absolute Nothingness. Preliminary Considerations on a Central Notion in the Philosophy of Nishida Kitarō and the Kyoto School," *MN* XXI/3-4, 1966, pp. 354–391.

Watts, Alan W. *The Way of Zen.* New York: New American Library, 1959, p. 224.

Wright, Arthur F. *Buddhism in Chinese History.* Stanford, Calif.: Stanford University Press, 1959, p. 144.

Wayman, Alex. "Concerning saṃdhābhāṣā/saṃdhibhāṣā/sandhyābhāṣā," MIMLR, pp. 789–796.

―――. "Contributions Regarding the Thirty Two Characteristics of the Great Person, Liebenthal Festschrift," *Sino-Indian Studies*, 5-3, May 1957, pp. 240–260.

———. *Analysis of the Śrāvakabhūmi Manuscript.* Univ. of California Publications in Classical Philosophy, 17, Berkeley & Los Angeles, 1961.

———. "A Report on the Śrāvaka-Bhūmi and its Author (Asaṅga)," JBRS, XLII (Nos 3-4, 1956), pp. 316-329.

——— and Hideko. trs. *The Lion's Roar of Queen Śrīmālā: A Buddhist Scripture on the Tathāgatagarbha Theory.* New York and London: Columbia University Press, 1974.

Weber, Max. *The Religion of China.* New York, 1964.

———. *The Religion of India.* Glencoe, Ill., 1958.

Wei Tat, tr. by. *Ch'eng Wei-shih Lun: The Doctrine of Mere Consciousness.* Hong Kong: The Ch'eng Wei-shih Lun Publication Committee, 1973.

Weinstein, Stanley. "The *Ālaya-vijñāna* in Early Yogācāra Buddhism," *Transactions of the International Conference of Orientalists in Japan,* vol. 3, 1958, pp. 46-58.

———. "Buddhism under the T'ang," draft chapter for Denis Twitchett, ed., *Sui and T'ang China,* 589-906, *Part II* (*The Cambridge History of China,* vol. 4). London, New York, and Melbourne: Cambridge University Press.

———. "The Concept of *Ālaya-vijñāna* in Pre-T'ang Chinese Buddhism," *Bukkyō shisōshi ronshū.* Tokyo: Daizō shuppan, 1964, pp. 33-50.

———. "Imperial Patronage in the Formation of T'ang Buddhism," in Denis Twitchett and Arthur F. Wright, eds., *Perspectives on the T'ang.* New Haven and London: Yale University Press, 1973, pp. 265-306.

Woodward, F. L. and E. M. Hare, trs. *The Book of Gradual Sayings,* 5 vols. London: Pali Text Society, 1961-1973.

———. "The Formation of the Sui Ideology," *Chinese Thought and Institution,* ed. J. K. Fairbank. Chicago, 1957.

——— et al., ed. *Perspectives on the T'ang.* New Haven, 1973.

Wright, Dale. "Emptiness and Paradox in the Thought of Fa-tsang" (Ph.D. dissertation), University of Iowa, 1980.

Wu, John C. H. *The Golden Age of Zen.* Taipei, Taiwan: United Publishing, 1975.

Yamada, James S. "The Tathāgata-garbha and the Collective Unconscious: A Two-Fingered Approach to Zen," *IBK*, 3, whole No. 6, March 1955, pp. 765-760.

Yampolski, Philip B. *The Platform Sutra of the Sixth Patriarch.* New York: Columbia University Press, 1967.

————, tr. by. *The Zen Master Hakuin: Selected Writings.* New York: Columbia University Press, 1971.

Yung, Hsi. *Buddhism and the Ch'an School of China.* Trans. by Chou Hsiang-Kuang; Indo-Chinese Literature Series, Allahabad, 1956.

Zaehner, R. C. *Mysticism, Sacred and Profane.* Oxford: Clarendon Press, 1957.

————. *Zen, Drugs and Mysticism.* New York: Vintage Books, 1974.

Zeuschner, Robert. "An Analysis of the Philosophical Criticisms of Northern Ch'an Buddhism" (Ph.D. dissertation), University of Hawaii, 1977.

Zürcher, E. *The Buddhist Conquest of China*, 2 vols. Leiden: E. J. Brill, 1959.

Index

salvation, 2, 11-13, 93
samādhi, 14, 106, 107, 121
Samantabhadra Bodhisattva,
100, 117
śamatha-vipaśyanā, 62, 63,
87, 88
sambhoga-kāya, 31
sāmbhogika-kāya, 31, 32
saṃgha, 86
samgwan, 133
saṃsāra, 42
saṃvṛti satya, 49-52
Schleiermacher, Freidrich
(1768-1834), 27
self-nature, 110
self-power (jiriki), 2, 46,
92-95
Seng-t'san (?-606), 122
She-lun, 119
Shen-hsiu (605?-706), 21-23
Song of Faith, 122
Sheng-mieh hsiang, 83
shih-chiao, 82
shih-hsin, 1
shih-shih wu-wi, 110
Shinran (1173-1262), 74, 93,
94, 96
Shōbōgenzō, 23, 56
skill-in-means (upāya), 51, 52,
114, 116
Sŏn. See Ch'an; Zen
śraddhā, 15, 16, 43, 64
Sthirmati, 32
storehouse consciousness, 127,
134
strong determination, 68
subject-object construction,
1, 35-38, 41, 42, 55, 56,
59, 141, 147
Suchness, 45, 48, 80, 83,
86-88, 99
sudden enlightenment and
gradual practice, 113
suddenness, 106
sudden practice, 57

sudden realization, 26
sudhana's journey, 115,
117-119
śūnyatā, 26, 31, 45, 50, 101
Suzuki, D. T., 39

Ta-ch'eng ch'i-hsin lun. See
Treatise on Awakening
Mahāyāna Faith
Ta-chih-tu lun, 3, 11, 12,
37, 38, 98
Ta-hui (1088-1163), 135, 136
Takasaki, Jikido, 29
Tao-sheng (360-434), 28, 29
Tahāgatagarbha, 29, 30
tathāgatagarbha-Pratityasam-
utpāda, 29, 30
thirty-two physical marks of
the Buddha, 32
three bodies theory (tri-kāya),
30, 31
three disciplines, 62, 63
three essentials, 67, 68, 124
three gates, 133, 134, 143
three greatnesses, 83-86, 88,
89, 99
Three Jewels (tri-ratna), 3, 86,
88, 99, 126
three levels of compassion, 98
Three-natures theory, 129, 132
Three Pillars of Zen, 67, 68
three stages of life, 70
Tillich, Paul, 69, 71-73, 142
ti-yung. See essence-function
construction
Tokiwa, Daijō, 29
t'ong pulgyo, 37
tono chŏmsu, 105
tranquilization, 87, 88
transformation, 43, 70, 107,
126-128, 130, 131
transformation body, 31-34
transformation of the basis.
See āśraya parāvṛtti
transmigration, 127, 129